The Darkness
"Talking"

OMNIBUS PRESS

THE DARKNESS *Talking*

Copyright © 2004 Omnibus Press
(A Division of Music Sales Limited)

Cover & Book designed by Fresh Lemon.
Picture research by Sarah Bacon.

ISBN: 1.84449.503.5
Order No: OP50413

The Author hereby asserts his/her right to be identified
as the author of this work in accordance with Sections 77 to 78 of the
Copyright, Designs and Patents Act 1988.

All rights reserved. No part of this book may be reproduced in
any form or by any electronic or mechanical means, including
information storage or retrieval systems, without permission in writing from
the publisher, except by a reviewer who may quote brief passages.

Exclusive Distributors:
Music Sales Limited,
8/9 Frith Street, London W1D 3JB, UK.

Music Sales Corporation,
257 Park Avenue South, New York, NY 10010, USA.

Macmillan Distribution Services,
53 Park West Drive, Derrimut, Vic 3030, Australia.

To the Music Trade only:
Music Sales Limited,
8/9 Frith Street, London W1D 3JB, UK.

Photo credits:
Front cover: Lex Van Rossen / Redferns

All inside images courtesy of LFI except:
Action Press / Rex Features: 109; Dave Allocca / Rex Features: 98; Simon Chapman: 87;
Rob Howarth / Rex Features: 71; Bob King / Redferns: 119; Angela Lubrano: 84, 89, 124;
Hayley Madden / Rex Features: 3, 61; Brian Rasic / Rex Features: 104;
Tim Rooke / Rex Features: 22; Sipa Press / Rex Features: 93; Mike Webster / Rex Features: 127

Colour Section Pic Credits: Simon Chapman: 8; Richard Ecclestone / Redferns: 2;
Tabatha Fireman / Redferns: 5; Peter Pakvis / Redferns: 7

Every effort has been made to trace the copyright holders of the
photographs in this book but one or two were unreachable.
We would be grateful if the photographers concerned would contact us.

Printed by: Caligraving Limited, Thetford, Norfolk.

A catalogue record for this book is available from the British Library.

Visit Omnibus Press on the web at www.omnibuspress.com

Introduction	6
Lowestoft	8
In The Beginning	12
Empire Building	14
Darkness Looming…	17
What's In A Name?	21
Making Their Way	23
Not Giving A Shuck	27
Heroes & Influences	32
The Music	36
Men On A Mission	52
Friends & NMEs	57
What D'ya Think?	65
The Brits	69
Sex, Drugs & Rock'n'Roll	73
Strutting Their Stuff…	77
Lights, Camera, Action	85
Catsuits & Lipstick	87
Just Justin	94
Brotherly Love	99
Ambition	101
Conquering America	103
Crowd Control	110
A Thing Called Fame	114
Famous Followers…	120
Future	125

CONTENTS

THE DARKNESS *Talking*

Supposedly, classic rock was wiped from the very face of the earth when Nirvana led the charge out of West Coast America in the early Nineties. No-one then thought the backlash, one decade on, would emanate from Lowestoft, a small town on the east coast of England. But so it's proved.

It all began for The Darkness with an appearance at Glastonbury 2003, for which they pocketed the princely sum of £75. From there, the band's fame snowballed to the extent that, a mere nine months later, their debut album *Permission To Land* had sold 1.2 million copies in the UK alone. Mixing the vocal gymnastics of Queen with the twin-guitar flash of Thin Lizzy, the pansticked stagecraft of Alice Cooper and the glossy harmonies of Def Leppard, The Darkness created a rock success story all their own.

Introduction

Yet outrageous frontman/guitarist Justin Hawkins, brother Dan, stone-faced bassist Frankie Poullain and all-action drummer Ed Graham had all paid their dues for longer than you'd think: they first got together several years earlier in a no-hope band called Empire, while Justin hid his light under a bushel as a keyboard-player before being persuaded to go out front. In many ways, it was fifth member Sue Whitehouse whose off-stage contribution kept the show on the road when spirits flagged. One-time fiancé Justin wrote the breakthrough song 'I Believe In A Thing Called Love' about her, but they announced their split in early 2004 – though she would, crucially, remain their manager.

From having opened the show at Glasto, the flamboyant foursome's triumphant return rested on whether the festival could now afford a band already making headway in the States and bidding to single-handedly lead a rock invasion. With three Brits under their arm and the unlikely endorsement of Prime Minister Tony Blair, who admitted borrowing their album from his children's record collection,
The Darkness seemed set for global domination.

In a world where rock seemed to be chasing its tail in ever-decreasing circles, it was refreshing to find a band painting in broad brush strokes – and one whose members seemed unafraid to speak their mind, both on and off the record. This collection of quotable quotes is only the beginning...

INTRODUCTION

THE DARKNESS *Talking*

Lowestoft

"People say are you a London band? And we say no because three-quarters of the people were brought up in Lowestoft. It's really important to remember that." JUSTIN

"My parents always talked about moving to New Zealand in case there was a nuclear fallout. They were quite hippyish in some ways but wanted us to grow up in the country and then leave the city stuff to our own choices later on. I wouldn't say that's done me any harm at all. I did find it a bit daunting moving to London, though, having been sheltered in that way." JUSTIN

"My earliest memory is drinking my own wee... My mum caught me drinking from my potty when I was a toddler. She gave me a smack too, so it was like a double punishment. I certainly wouldn't ever do that again!" JUSTIN

"The last thing we need is some kind of 'heavy metal noise' (moving in). It would spoil the town's character."

SOUTHWOLD RESIDENTS

"It's all very well Eminem going on about Detroit. You have to be a bit braver to go around singing the praises of Lowestoft." JUSTIN

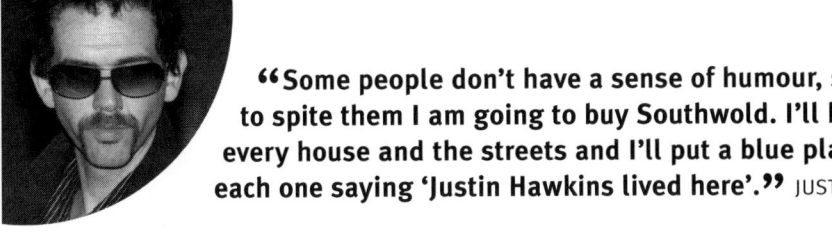

"Some people don't have a sense of humour, so just to spite them I am going to buy Southwold. I'll buy every house and the streets and I'll put a blue plaque on each one saying 'Justin Hawkins lived here'." JUSTIN

"I suppose it's always been wonderful (being their Mum) but a bit different now. You have to pinch yourself because it's really gathered speed. Because we've lived here a while the neighbours are aware (of their fame) and they've watched it grow, so it's been fine. We had about half a dozen fans hanging around (outside) the house over Christmas, but Dan's in Jamaica and Justin came Christmas Day and then shot off. I got recognised in the bank yesterday. They went, 'Oh, I saw you on TV! You're Ma Hawkins!'"
SANDY HAWKINS, MOTHER OF THE BAND'S JUSTIN AND DAN

"The boys talk about Lowestoft a lot. Frank gets quite upset because he comes from Scotland." SANDY HAWKINS

"They did say they'd build us a swimming pool (when they made it). It could be a little inflatable £5.99 thing with a pump. We'll wait and see what Santa brings in a parcel. But no, we haven't got a swimming pool yet!" SANDY HAWKINS, XMAS 2003

"It's long deserved – it's been 10 years' slog. Once they are famous, people lose perspective. It didn't happen overnight, but the starving and sleeping on people's floors is forgotten. They are already conquering America. The world's their oyster."
SANDY HAWKINS

"At the beginning it makes you a bit nervous about whether they're going to pull it off or not. But now you know they're going to pull it off, it's all right." FATHER HARRY HAWKINS

"I think they have been a great asset to the town. They are very, very popular with the kids. It's great news for the town. It's sometimes seen as the back of beyond but Lowestoft can still produce very talented people. I'm chuffed as monkeys."
MAYOR TERRY KELLY

LOWESTOFT

THE DARKNESS *Talking*

"It's amazing – I'm from Lowestoft, this time last year I'd hardly been to any countries at all and now we've been round the world."

JUSTIN

"My Dad said, 'cos he's a builder... he sees (a rock critic) as somebody trying to affect our career. So he said 'When you know that character is in the pub, tell me, and I'll fucking take his head off!' I was like 'Nice one Dad. Last time I heard you swear was when I was eleven and that was bleeding.' But he obviously feels very strongly about it because it's his boys' careers." **JUSTIN**

"People around here are quite surprised that we admit to being from around here. There is one other band I can think of who became very high profile and insisted they were from Leeds, though the crux of the band spent a long time gigging in these parts. Even though I was born in Chertsey, Surrey, I still consider East Anglia my home.

"We were as disappointed as anyone (not to play Lowestoft) but as I said in the press conference there isn't a venue where it's appropriate. This show has to be a certain size, capacity and it's all about the technical specs we need. There aren't venues like that in Lowestoft.

"I used to go swimming at the venue we're playing (a sports centre in Great Yarmouth) because it's got a wave machine as opposed to Lowestoft which doesn't." **JUSTIN**

"There's an intense rivalry between two the two towns (Lowestoft and Yarmouth). People in Lowestoft have been asking when we're going to play a show there, but all the venues have been closed down or turned into bingo halls. It's very strange that people are up in arms about it. We've never played there before anyway!"

JUSTIN

"I expect it'll be like when we turned up in Nottingham the other day and some bloke said, 'Oh it's that cunt out of The Darkness'. If I'd gone to Lowestoft this time last year it would've been, 'Oh, there's that cunt from school! Get a haircut, soap-dodger!'" **JUSTIN**

"I won first prize for lead-miniature painting at Lowestoft Model Fair." ED

"We've still got that contrary nature which dictates that if anyone wants us to tone things down we're just going to turn it up. It's tempting to go global now but I'd still rather sing about Lowestoft than the Sunset Strip." JUSTIN

LOWESTOFT

THE DARKNESS *Talking*

In The Beginning

"Phil Spencer, my history teacher, was really supportive of the music when I was at school. Even though he taught me history, he really showed an interest in it, and I haven't seen him since I was at school and I'm looking forward to hooking up with him again. I don't know if he's even heard the album..." JUSTIN

"Him and his wife used to drive 'his and hers' Morris Minors. School's an important part of my life and that guy's just shat all over it. If I'm in my monster truck and I come across a fucking Morris Minor I'm going to fucking plough through that fucker. Ha ha! What a cunt."

JUSTIN, ON THE HEADMASTER WHO SOLD HIS PHOTO TO THE SUN

"You have to spend a certain amount of time in your bedroom practising your guitar. You can't hang out and be cool. That's why geeks are better musicians." JUSTIN

"After school, I moved to London to get involved in music. I couldn't imagine doing anything else. I took the whole thing seriously from a very young age. All I wanted to do was form a band." DAN

"In the early days it was, 'Well, at least your girlfriend's got a proper job!' It's hard to justify it because there's such a small chance of making it. But at the end of the day everyone's been really supportive. We're quite a liberal family really in that everyone just does what makes them happy. As long as you're happy, they're happy." JUSTIN

"My father's very good at saying 'fuck off' to people. That's where I get it from – it's one of the things I've got to thank him for." JUSTIN

"I knew from an early age exactly what I wanted to do. I wanted to be a musician and that was it. It made life a lot easier knowing what I was aiming for. I taught myself how to play the guitar and I just knew that was what I wanted to do as my career. I was on a mission."
DAN

"When I started learning the guitar I had lessons for a year. After that year passed I was better than the guitar teacher. He'd tell me to practise for half an hour every day, but I'd be doing three or four hours. That's how you end up being *really* fucking good." JUSTIN

"I lost interest in playing in bands for a while because music became a bit of a shitty thing. Grunge was depressing. I like Nirvana, but everything that happened after it was rubbish, so I decided I wanted to learn about music technology and computers and acoustics. I ended up going to Huddersfield to do a BTEC."
JUSTIN

"We started in the pubs. I was playing in pubs when I was 15 – I probably shouldn't admit that – I'm 28 now, so it's been 13 years in the making. The idea is you do the pubs and then you go and do the clubs, theatres, arenas, stadiums, festivals. If you don't have that elbow-grease mentality and do the stuff in the early days then you get caught out when you go up a level. We've gone up several levels in a short period of time because we've done the preparation and we're ready for it." JUSTIN

IN THE BEGINNING

THE DARKNESS *Talking*

Empire Building

"I answered an ad that Dan had put in the music press. That's when we met and from then on we were sharing flats and trying to get something together. But when Justin came back from college, he wasn't so keen on being in a band with Dan." FRANKIE

"People kept telling us to tone it down. But if anything that made us go the opposite way. If someone suggested Frankie trimmed his moustache, he'd grow it longer." DAN

"The thing with most bands is that it's more about fucking politics than anything else. I don't like people very much so I couldn't be arsed with it. I joined (Empire) in the end but at that time I was just the synthesiser player." JUSTIN

"I mixed a track for Empire about six years ago. They were a bit indie to be honest, but they rocked. That's when I became friends with them. We had the same interest and liked the same music. Somehow I knew they'd be successful one day."
PRODUCER/SOUND ENGINEER PEDRO FERREIRA

"I did backing vocals (in Empire) that had to be higher than the main bloke's because I was harmonising with him and he was quite a high singer. It's the loudest part of my voice. In any rehearsal environment, you can get yourself heard by screaming." JUSTIN

"We all went to school together. We've all known each other for years and we all moved to London about five or six years ago. Justin, Dan and Frank were in another band called Empire and they kicked out their singer. They were looking for a new singer for about two years.

"Dan and Justin's aunt owns a pub in Norfolk. One New Year's Eve (1999) Justin was doing karaoke along with star jumps and dancing. His brother said he was a natural performer and that he should be a singer, so the idea came on Millennium Eve and it went from there." ED

"We never had a proper direction in Empire. To start with we had an incredible singer but it just didn't work out the way we wanted it to, so we sacked him. We split up because we spent too long looking for a new frontman. Justin had a shot at singing, but because the music was much more downbeat it didn't really work." FRANKIE

"We had unnecessarily high standards which didn't help. You've got to be able to start somewhere. When Empire split, Frankie went to live in Venezuela, Ed was at college in Salisbury, I think, and Justin was making a living doing radio jingles. It wasn't a great time, I must admit." DAN

"Originally, we just played as much as possible and earned a following via word-of-mouth. Along the way we've assembled a kick-ass team who do all of our promotional stuff." JUSTIN

EMPIRE BUILDING

THE DARKNESS Talking

"Our first gig was at a friend's funeral." DAN

"Justin was dead ordinary really. He loved to produce cheesy music, he was into electronic pop, never metal. We were one of the first colleges to offer this kind of course. He gained distinctions in various modules including one in self-management and development."
RICK COCKER, JUSTIN'S TUTOR

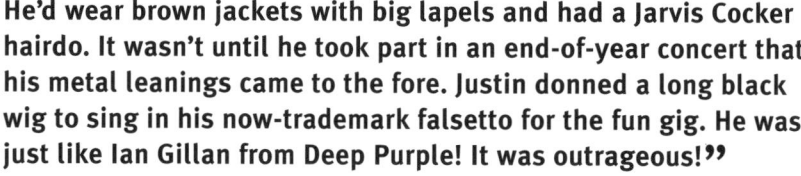

"Justin dressed a bit like Austin Powers, or Mike Flowers, the spoof Sixties singer. He'd wear brown jackets with big lapels and had a Jarvis Cocker hairdo. It wasn't until he took part in an end-of-year concert that his metal leanings came to the fore. Justin donned a long black wig to sing in his now-trademark falsetto for the fun gig. He was just like Ian Gillan from Deep Purple! It was outrageous!"
CHARLIE GRIFFITHS, MUSIC TECHNOLOGY LECTURER

"I didn't even recognise Justin when I saw The Darkness on TV. I saw them on *Later With Jools Holland* with this amazing singer who jumped on to the top of a grand piano, then leapt to the ground as the song ended. I thought they were brilliant. Then three days later, in college, someone said to me 'Did you see Justin?' I couldn't believe it." **SARAH HUTTON, JUSTIN'S MUSIC BUSINESS TUTOR**

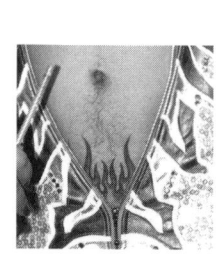

Darkness Looming...

"Ed went to school with Dan and Jus, and they played in bands together when they were younger... I met Dan in London seven years ago. We played in quite a few different bands, always hiring and firing people. That's one thing in common is we're both very ambitious, and Justin was always the kind of guy who didn't like to take himself very seriously, so that was one hurdle we had to overcome. Dan and Justin are the opposite in many ways.

"I went to Venezuela for nine months, jungle trekking round there, and then I got an e-mail from Justin saying, 'We're starting this band called the Darkness' – which then I thought was a terrible name, but which I've since grown to love." **FRANKIE**

"Despite what you may have read, I didn't reveal my singing talents at a karaoke night. It was just a family party on Millennium Eve." JUSTIN

DARKNESS LOOMING...

THE DARKNESS *Talking*

"We were all getting pissed, and Justin and I were laughing at our dad dancing. Then Justin did this turn, basically singing and doing contemporary dance to 'Bohemian Rhapsody' – it was the funniest thing I've ever seen. But at the same time I was nodding my head and smiling and rocking. It was the same reaction that people get when they see us for the first time. Straight away we decided to form this band." DAN

"I used to do backing vocals in the bands we were in before so I think everyone knew I could sing – it just hadn't made as much sense before. At first I didn't want to play the guitar as well because I didn't want to be restricted, but Dan talked me into it." JUSTIN

"My brother was a bit of a beach bum, and he worked with this tour company in Venezuela, taking students around the mountains. I went over to help out and ended up staying. I'd just finished when I got an e-mail from Dan and Justin saying that they'd decided to get something together." FRANKIE

"Before this I was in poppy bands, so I played more melodic parts. I had to completely change the way I play to make it heavy enough for this band. That said, our drummer Ed and I like to play as heavy as we can but still leave enough room for the other two guys. I just do my best to glue the drums and band together." FRANKIE

"We used to rehearse at Dan and Justin's parents' house. They had an outside toilet block and their dad is a builder and he converted the outside toilet into a rehearsal room. It was a pub years and years ago. Thankfully it didn't smell..." ED

"We sent him (Frankie) a message saying, 'We're assembling a unit and we're looking for a bassist.' We got this cynical reply saying, 'I expect you're only considering me because I did all that work trying to find a singer last time...' So we had to mail him back to say that no, we *really* wanted him to do it." JUSTIN

"I'd moved to London a bit earlier with the intent to join a band. The first one I joined was Q*Sling. My housemate introduced me to them and I was in the band for six months, but then these guys asked me to join them. Even though I was friends with Q*Sling, I had to go with my oldest friends." ED

"We're really close. We'd been at school and been in bands together, so we had a good feeling about the whole thing. We booked ourselves into this crappy rehearsal room in Acton and it was obvious that it was going to be really good." DAN

"If it was a band with just Justin in it, or just Dan, I don't think I'd want to be in it. There's a balance between them musically that just works." ED

"The Darkness are four men, men's men. Your basic macho, masculine, testosterone-driven, muscular, tall, handsome, chiselled, square-jawed, large-chinned men. Three of whom are from Lowestoft. One is Scottish." JUSTIN

DARKNESS LOOMING...

" THE DARKNESS *Talking*

"We've all known each other for a long time, and I think if you get four people in a room, it creates a certain ambience... But that shapes a lot of things; if one of those people were different, the whole atmosphere would be different." ED

"You're talking about chemistry – that secret ingredient that keeps the Frosties crunchy at the end of the fucking bowl. No-one knows what it is. But, to a certain extent, there's no point finding out, because Frosties do what Frosties do. If you want to craft your own breakfast-cereal, then find your own magic ingredient. That's what I'm saying: you can't buy what we've got." JUSTIN

"We spent a long time just messing about and being unfocused. But as soon as we became focused we knew it was going to happen, at the end of the day – and, excuse the cliché, but cream always rises to the top." FRANKIE

"We have been going for years and the relationships in this band are long-term, so it's not like we have just been thrust into the spotlight. We have done hundreds of gigs since 2000. So we see it as a curve that has gone steadily upwards in terms of the following we had, and then with the recent exposure we have had recently it's gone up." JUSTIN

"I think it's because we've been very thorough. We cover all bases. We've got four very different personalities in this band, but the chemistry is perfect. In a nutshell, maybe it's been about talent, balls and personality!" FRANKIE

What's In A Name?

"We were looking for a name, and we were so (annoyed) we couldn't come up with something decent that we went for the worst thing we could find. In a way, it's the perfect thing for us because the second you hear the music and hear the name, people put the two together and say, 'Why?' Within five seconds of hearing the band, they're asking themselves, 'Why are they called The Darkness?'"

DAN

"I think all music comes from the Darkness at some point. It's a nagging need to express something and it's usually caused by something your mind or something you need to get of your chest. That's The Darkness for me – it is an antidote to something... or is it an expression of something?" JUSTIN

"One day someone's going to connect everything – the name of the band, The Darkness, to the name of the album, to the air stewardess to the spaceship – we're not intelligent enough to do it at the moment! There isn't a logic there but there is *something* that holds it together – who knows what it is?" ED

WHAT'S IN A NAME?

THE DARKNESS Talking

❝Maybe we could get Stephen Hawking to work it out...❞ DAN

❝That was a silly in-joke that got out of hand. Now I keep reading about my 'serious depression'. It's absolute bollocks.❞
ED ON REPORTS THAT THE DARKNESS WAS NAMED AFTER HIS STATE OF MIND

❝We call ourselves The Darkness, a name that even our friends said we'd never get anywhere with because... it's nice to have a challenge. It's a handicap. 'Cos otherwise it's not fair on the rest of music. Ha ha!❞ JUSTIN

❝The truth is that we tried to find the most inappropriate name known to man. And somehow we've grown into it!❞ JUSTIN

Making Their Way

"A demo tape landed on my desk and, for some reason, I listened to it straight away rather than throwing it in the box. I called them up and went to see them in rehearsal and we hit it off immediately. For me, having solid relationships is very important. I'm very instinctive about the people I choose to work with."

MANAGER SUE WHITEHOUSE

"Right from the start, (Whitehouse) was getting us gigs, which is quite hard in the beginning. In London, you'd think it would be quite easy because there are so many venues but we had challenges. All the best things about us worked against us. (Working with Whitehouse) is all based on trust – and that's very, very important." JUSTIN

"When we started off it was high impact and some fairly dodgy costumes and songs. It took a year to sound exciting and another to sound crafted and have good songs." DAN

MAKING THEIR WAY

THE DARKNESS *Talking*

"A year ago the shit really hit the fan, didn't it? We fine-tuned it and now the shit's stopped hitting the fan. The blades have been worn down to almost nothing, there's no need to duck any more – we'll just take it full on in the face." JUSTIN

"We've put a lot of groundwork in. There's a lot of people out there who have seen us once somewhere in a pub or heard our songs late at night on radio and so on and so forth. We've done four years of it before we'd even released a single on a (proper) record label. It's put us in good stead and that's why we're ready for all this stuff." DAN

"People are initially shocked and think, 'How can this be serious?' But if you come to a few gigs you realise it's not a joke, they're proper songs just delivered in a different way. The bottom line is that we mean it." DAN

"The studio (Chapel Studios in Lincolnshire) was cheap and cheerful and the food was outstanding. The people were lovely. They couldn't do enough for us. It all took place away from the heady attractions of not having any money in London. We recorded the album using my money. Yes, I am slightly bitter about it, but then I'm slightly bitter about being Number 1. Like, why didn't that happen three years ago, you cunts?" JUSTIN

"In the early days, when we were just releasing independent singles, there wasn't that much to write about. But we'd get a good single review, and that'd lead to a great live review. We got a lot of interest early on." DAN

> "We worked really, really hard in those days. We still do. A lot of bands will play a gig and then maybe spend a couple of months going 'Oh, maybe we should write some more stuff'. We were at it all the time. We rehearsed what we had a lot rather than changing our sound." JUSTIN

> "We sent a demo to the festival people (South By Southwest Music Festival) and they said that out of the thousands of demos they'd received it was the best one. That was pretty refreshing, especially when they invited us over (to Texas) and paid for our accommodation." JUSTIN

> "It's all kicking off now, and about time, too – we've been working at this for years." JUSTIN

> "Justin got the Mesa/Boogie (amplifier) endorsement by ringing up and soloing down the phone." DAN

> "It's funny, we've never made any attempt in our songs to be global – I mean, we sing about stuff that happens in Lowestoft, for God's sake. But I think Americans, and anyone else for that matter, can relate to it and are getting into it." JUSTIN

> "What we could always fall back on (in the early days) is we had such a great time at the gigs. When you've got that, you can quite effectively go 'Fuck everyone, because we're having a good time.' They're so fashion-based in London, everything is pulled apart and criticised and that's not what we're about. Our music isn't there to be over-analysed; it's there to be enjoyed. It's worked out all right for us in the end. People are obviously ready for a change." JUSTIN

> "We were always a legendary band and people came to see us out of curiosity. It wasn't big and it wasn't clever but we kept on doing it. Then it became fashionable and when that dies out we'll still be here behaving like bell ends. The Hoxtonites will die out, if they haven't already." JUSTIN

MAKING THEIR WAY

THE DARKNESS Talking

"We're Gibson artists now. We went in before we were signed and told them we'd just played South by South West (annual festival in Texas) and we'd really like some Les Pauls. They said 'You can't just come in here! We don't do stuff like that unless you're front-page material!' While we were in the office, *Music Week* arrived and they opened it up and they were like 'Oh, The Darkness. South By South West. Okay, lads, nice one.' They're been really supportive ever since. Mesa/Boogie endorses us. For the last couple of years Marshall has helped too." JUSTIN

"We almost have a name for ourselves as the band that opens all the festivals. A big part of our rise to prominence is to do with word of mouth. In T in the Park people said we had a bigger crowd than R.E.M. the night before. The crowd went right back to the hot-dog stands at the back, so it's worked out quite well. Saying that, at Glastonbury it was quite hard having cameras in our faces so early in the morning." FRANKIE

"We've been doing this project with this line-up for two years now, it's just that the songwriting has become more developed and everyone's roles have become more defined." JUSTIN

"For T in the Park and Glastonbury it was the same band who followed us: Echo & The Bunnymen. Someone overheard them saying 'Oh no, we're after the Darkness again!'

"I guess in a way it can be tough coming after us: it's not the same as Electric Six and it's not the same as all those garage bands, it's something different. We're just doing our own thing – that can sound pretty big-headed, can't it?" FRANKIE

Not Giving A Shuck

"Is this a face of concern? No, it definitely isn't a face that gives a toss what anyone thinks. We wouldn't have done this if we were concerned about how people responded to it. It's great fun for us." **FRANKIE**

"The only things we don't take seriously is ourselves as people. In terms of writing songs, performing, recording, we take it all very seriously. But because we don't take ourselves very seriously as people we're often mistaken as being a joke band, as being a novelty, gimmicky. That was in the early days in (the United Kingdom), but we've converted pretty much the majority in this country because we've got all the ingredients, the songs, to be a great band.

"We got a lot of advice in the industry telling us to ditch this or ditch that. Justin was told to get rid of his tattoos, and I was told to shave off my moustache. That was just at the superficial level, but there were many more things in which we were told to represent ourselves in a much more serious way. We refused to do that." **FRANKIE**

NOT GIVING A SHUCK

THE DARKNESS *Talking*

"We crack on and do what we do. You can't let (criticism) affect you, really. You judge a man by his enemies and whatever you're doing that's causing them to dislike you, the people who like you are going to like you more if you keep doing it. You can't turn your back on something that's good and even if people tell you it's not good, it won't stop you. There's the people who were like, 'Oh, I could have signed them years ago.' We're like, 'No you *couldn't* have. You're a cunt and we've always thought you were a cunt.'" JUSTIN

"I don't like the *Sun* saying 'He's got bad teeth'. But I think 'Yeah, so?' They're white but they're really fucked-up and sharp and that's fine – that's the way I like them. But at the same time it's not a musical criticism, so... now I don't really give a shit what anyone says." JUSTIN

"We are here to annoy people. Just when you think we're gone, we are going to be there, up your arse. All the time. We are going to be in your pub. You go home to try to escape, you can switch on the radio, the TV and we are going to be there. We are going to hound and harass you." FRANKIE

"People that say we're a shit band haven't listened to our music. They don't like the image, and may find something unpalatable about a man wearing the sort of stuff that I wear. 'I don't really know where to look,' they may say to themselves. 'I feel a bit inadequate.' And they let that get in the way of the fact that we are a brilliant band. They are wrong, and we all know it." JUSTIN

"We don't read the papers, we just don't have time. We're not going to force the issue, none of us have sought any professional help yet but it might happen one day! We all know each other very well and we all keep things quite light-hearted, we can take it all with a pinch of salt." FRANKIE

"Everyone who works with us is saying 'fuck off' to the music industry. We're all motivated by the fact that we're all kicking arse together as a team." JUSTIN

"It's men's rock with balls, and that never goes out of fashion. People either seem to like us or strongly hate us, but the balance of power is shifting. People in high places are beginning to appreciate The Darkness." JUSTIN

"When I see things that are totally inaccurate or people don't get it, I do feel sorry for them in a way. I think to myself, 'You're one of those people that should be working in the dole office.'" DAN

"I want people to remember me as a person who just didn't give a fuck, one of the true 'not give a fuckers' in this world." JUSTIN

"Occasionally, you get an inspired piece of journalism. Like on Teletext, which described us as 'delusional twerps'. I can live with that. It's genius writing. I'm just pleased it wasn't published on Ceefax." JUSTIN

"We've always had our knockers and our ups and downs in this industry. You know, but we've got to know the ins and outs, and it's very easy to get screwed in this game. We've learnt the hard way."
JUSTIN

"The (press) misconstrued us as being a non-hit wonder. In terms of being misunderstood, you have some people that interpret it as being glam-rock and then people seeing it as a horrible, Andrew WK-type thing." JUSTIN

NOT GIVING A SHUCK

THE DARKNESS *Talking*

"I think we like proving people wrong. It doesn't really matter how people perceive the music or the show." DAN

"I think in a strange kind of way I know we're really popular and probably the biggest band in the country at the moment, but at the same time there is this real cult thing going on. The people that actually get us really love us because they get us and because the people that don't get us hate us so much. There's always gonna be that love 'em or hate 'em, although it seems to be a much larger percentage who love us now." DAN

"We stand alone. We had to struggle for years, a lot of people had a thing against us. We've done it ourselves; we're not part of a scene, and I don't think we ever will be." FRANKIE

"Some of the record companies that were sniffing around would say stuff like, 'How can I be sure that you're not being ironic? How can I market you?' It's just paranoia and ignorance. If you don't like the music, fuck off. Go and drive a bus. This is the entertainment trade, and you need to be entertaining people. If you're not doing that... fuck off and work in a library, you twat." JUSTIN

"Obviously we don't see ourselves as cheesy or we wouldn't be wasting all this time working really fucking hard to fight against the grain." FRANKIE

"When we came out in the UK we were dividing people. And I think it's definitely normal for a band like us to have that response. It's never going to be unanimously positive, there'll always be people who hate us. But that's good, in a way." JUSTIN

"We're so different to everything else around that it's taken hard work to get here. People say it's not what you do it's who you know – and that's not true either. We've got friends in the music trade and that hasn't helped us at all. We're a phenomenon because people didn't want us to exist when we do." JUSTIN

"I think we're an improvement on sliced bread!" JUSTIN

THE DARKNESS *Talking*

Heroes & Influences

> "I was doing Music Technology and there was a pop course running concurrently with it. So I opted to doing some modules from that because I thought it would boost my CV, as it were. We actually ended up doing some gigs as the band in (Deep Purple) style and it was totally natural for me. The course was run by people who were deeply disillusioned and it was really a case of those who can, do, and those who can't, teach!

> "I think in a way what they were trying to was mould the future so they still had an interest in the scene themselves. But if I would have been at college now and it would have been a module on the sound of Limp Bizkit I wouldn't have even bothered with it in the first place – that thought's just *so* worrying!" **JUSTIN**

> "**I was talking about the whole Dad-rock thing; it's incredibly clichéd, the way that Noel Gallagher or Ian McCulloch (Echo & The Bunnymen) write their lyrics – apart from maybe their first records – yet, they're given that kind of credibility, an indie-credibility. It is farcical really. They're not taking any risks. Oasis are a decent rock-band, but I was making the point that Justin's lyrics in relation to such a style are very underrated.**" FRANKIE

> "I don't think (rock and metal) ever went away, I think its more to do with the fact that we've become a really good band – I mean, Maiden will always go in high in the charts because they're a strong band. As much as I'd like to think that old-school rock will make a comeback, I don't think its happening right now and think we're still out their on our own in a lot of ways... I'd love to see those type of bands – hard rock, pop-metal kind of bands – come back around again, though." **DAN**

❝I don't know how to do that Fleetwood Mac thing very well where there's a solo that you sing along to. I'm the sort of solo player where you go dibblydibblydibbly-wub-wub, whereas Dan does like a fanfare thing.❞ JUSTIN

❝(Late Thin Lizzy frontman) Phil Lynott's daughter's a fan of ours, she was on the guest-list for one of our shows.❞ DAN

❝None of us have bought an album by a new band in 10 years.❞ DAN

❝Our influences are Aerosmith, and in particular Steven Tyler – he changed my life back in '89 – while AC/DC have provided years of inspiration.❞ JUSTIN

❝I remember when *Pump* by Aerosmith came out. That kind of rock was really dying off them, but it had always appealed to me. I'd be wearing tight jeans to school and had long hair and people used to say to me, 'Who the hell do you think you are?'❞ JUSTIN

❝I know it's nothing like our album, but *Pump* by Aerosmith would be (my favourite), I like the fact that the last track is a ballad. The album is all about sexual enjoyment and having a good time, but it ends with a sentimental ballad that's saying, 'I'm very sensitive and I'd like you to come back.' Before the last track it's all about shagging and dancing!❞ JUSTIN

HEROES & INFLUENCES

THE DARKNESS *Talking*

"Our influences? Anything by Thin Lizzy. The second the guitars started pairing off and playing together the tennis racket would come out. But we were lucky enough that there were always guitars around the house, so we didn't have to air guitar. That makes a difference, I think, between being a fan and a musician." DAN

"I would have two fantasy bands – dead and alive... The dead band would be fronted by Bon Scott, John Bonham on drums, Jimi Hendrix and Paul Kossoff (lead and rhythm) and Phil Lynott on bass.

"A live band would be fronted by Steve Tyler, Tommy Lee on drums, Angus and Malcolm Young on the guitars. I think I'd play bass, just so I could say I'd performed with those guys!"

JUSTIN

"My elder brother's record collection – he was into Deep Purple and Pink Floyd and Rush – had a lot of heavy rock and prog rock, Seventies kind of stuff." FRANKIE

"We had a great time on the Def Leppard tour – it was a real honour to have been invited and I hope we made a few friends along the way." JUSTIN

"(Fleetwood Mac's) Lindsey Buckingham was my favourite lead guitar player and that's what I base my lead on." DAN

" What I used to listen to as a child was stuff like Fleetwood Mac and Queen through my dad. When I developed my own taste it was Aerosmith and Van Halen. There ain't a lot of it around! It's a return to our roots, really, rather than swim with the other fishes – make your own pool. " JUSTIN

" It's only recently that I've tried to get a grip with what's happening on the scene. Generally speaking I only listen to what I like to listen to. Sometime I feel raped by the hype if I buy an album that's supposed to be great and it's not. For my money I think that the great music is from yesteryear. People don't really make proper albums any more, do they? " JUSTIN

" We're not steeped in nostalgia. If it's new and it sounds good we'll play it. I've just bought a Gretsch Elliot Easton signature model, made on the specifications of the guitarist from The Cars. It's phenomenal. " DAN

" Rock music is kicking arse again – it's a sign of the times that the forthcoming Bon Jovi, AC/DC, Aerosmith and Kiss tours are among the most anticipated music events for ages. People are beginning to cherish the old values and, thanks to Busted, nu-metal is croaking its last death rattle even as we speak. With a bit of luck, The Darkness will be driving the next bandwagon that everybody jumps on – but don't forget, we were around before classic rock was fashionable and we'll still be around when it goes out again. " JUSTIN

" We thought that people would just bite our hands off because, for me in particular, everything I've ever listened to has been about frontmen with showmanship, quality guitar solos, proper players and mean songs. But it's only been since bands like The Datsuns have come around that the industry has shifted to bands like ourselves. If you think about the turn of the millennium and what was around? Richard Ashcroft was having his solo thing and the singer-songwriter Jeff Buckley obsessives. " JUSTIN

HEROES & INFLUENCES

THE DARKNESS *Talking*

The Music

"We don't try to follow any formulas in our songwriting; we just try to come up with things that excite us and make us smile. If we did follow a formula, we wouldn't have those ten distinctive songs on the album. Sure, we take inspiration from a lot of different areas, but then we take it somewhere else. 'Black Shuck', for instance, starts off with an AC/DC-type riff, but then we take it into a blues chorus about drinking whiskey and shagging women, and then turn it into something medieval to keep it fresh." FRANKIE

"**People are going to shit themselves when they hear us. Frankie's bass lines oscillate at a frequency that increases bowel movements. So go to the toilet before we come on – that way you won't have any accidents.**" JUSTIN

"As far as I'm concerned, it's all about the band's chemistry. You can have the most technically proficient individual players in the world, but if the chemistry isn't there, it isn't worth a shit. I mean, there are spots on our album where things speed up and slow down, but you can't question our chemistry." FRANKIE

"**It's all about the songs and we're really big on songwriting and getting the best arrangements we can. Once you've got the songs you can do whatever you want.**" DAN

"When you have detractors, especially in the band's infancy, it must have been tempting for others at a similar stage to do some Turin Brakes-y type stuff, because it's popular. But we've never been like that – we just do what we do, and if you don't like it you are wrong, and you'll find out eventually that you are wrong. And you can only apologise to yourself so much, having forfeited the time to really enjoy music." JUSTIN

“I think people are sick of that whole smoothed-over, auto-tuned, synchronised stuff. I suppose there's a lesson in the fact that the White Stripes and us put out two of this year's cheapest albums to make, but have had so much success.” FRANKIE

“I do insist on writing my own lyrics: I don't think I could do it if someone else was writing them and they were bad. I tried to write about heroin addiction loads of times: I know people who have issues with that, but it's difficult if you're not the perpetrator.”
JUSTIN

“All the rhythm guitars, bass and drums were played live and all the guitar solos, piano, organ and all the vocals were overdubbed. They're excellent guitarists – the solos didn't take long at all to do. 'Holding My Own' has got three of Justin's solos, and on 'Love Is Only A Feeling' we had Dan playing 13 acoustic guitar lines, so obviously it was overdubbed! There wasn't much editing; we took care to get really good takes.”
PEDRO FERREIRA

THE MUSIC

THE DARKNESS *Talking*

"Things have changed, but not dramatically. We're doing the same stuff we did a couple of years ago but without worrying too much about things. It's happening now – the ball's rolling, so it's just a case of trying to keep up with the ball rather than pushing it."
JUSTIN

"I'm having a pedalboard made that can run six amps. Because we're going to play bigger venues soon. I'm looking at having six separate amps running. I've got a Wizard on order, but you can't even try one out beforehand, there's no shop over here. I won't see it for nine months and I won't know what it's like. I can't wait, though, because Malcolm Young uses them. All the time I've known AC/DC he's mixed a Wizard with a Super 100, which is one of the ones I've got. You know, I would have made the most amazing guitar tech... but fuck that!" DAN

"We're like your favourite meal, maybe a pasta dish. The spaghetti is our rock side, the sauce is our metal side and the Parmesan is our pop side." FRANKIE

"There's a quality leap between any other guitar and Gibson, which is the top. I've never got into Fenders – even though some of their designs look cool, they're a bit too twangy and a bit too country, and they really don't have the balls the Les Paul facilitates. Another thing about the Les Paul is the carpentry involved – somebody spent a long time crafting those babies, and it's an honour and a privilege to pick up a piece of wood that's been manipulated in that way." JUSTIN

"A lot of times, I come in with some music and we go from there; but, sometimes, the lyrics don't happen – if Justin's not inspired to sing on it, it gets dumped and we work on something new. We've got a lot to choose from. It comes from different guises. We can write on acoustics around the table. It doesn't always start with a riff, or us just kicking arse right away – the songs go through a lot of stages in their development." DAN

"I think kids are a lot more open to that sort of thing than people realise. A lot of these kids will come to see us because they've seen us through the pop media, like *Top Of The Pops* and *CD:UK* etc. It's probably a whole new thing for them, their first rock show." DAN

"We're so popular because we cover all the bases. So many other bands, whether through complacency or taste or trying to fit in don't, and you only get one aspect." ED

"We recorded the album over two weeks. At the beginning I was trying to do 11am to 1am, but towards the end it was almost 24 hours a day. It was a lot of fun, but it's always a bit stressful when you're making these things. I'm quite a perfectionist, but we've got a really good relationship." PEDRO FERREIRA

"People think we appeal to the lowest common denominator and the high-brow. But I think we have an appeal to everyone in between, too. Everyone across the board." JUSTIN

"I think it takes a lot of balls to do what we do and I think if anyone tried to copy the way we do stuff I think they'd seriously struggle to pull it off. Our audiences are getting younger and younger. We had a signing session in Dublin recently and one of the kids must have been about 12!

"A lot of these kids haven't heard of the bands we were influenced by, but hopefully one day they might go out and buy some of the stuff we listened to, AC/DC, ZZ Top etc. So who knows? In five years' time, maybe a lot of kids who are really into the stuff we're into will go out and start making music like them." DAN

THE MUSIC

THE DARKNESS *Talking*

I Believe In A Thing Called Love

"The first EP ('I Believe In A Thing Called Love') is totally sold out – not even worth trying to find that one! 'Get Your Hands Off My Woman' is still around – the one to go for is our next single, 'Growing On Me' which is out on the 9th June 2003. I want that motherfucker in the charts." JUSTIN

"A lot of bands today try to be edgy and cryptic about (love) and never actually say the word, but the word says more than anything else." JUSTIN

"It began as 'one of those things that makes you laugh like we shouldn't be doing this' but later, we worked it out with the band. It was so obvious it's a good song that we saw it through to completion." DAN

Get Your Hands Off My Woman

"When we did 'Get Your Hands Off...' as a single, and it went to Number 43, which was above all our expectations – with no poster campaign or anything, and bear in mind it features the word 'motherfucker' eight times and the word 'cunt' twice – this guy at *The Guardian* said (adopts gravelly voice), 'They almost infringed on the Top 40 and, based on this performance, I can't see them going much better than that...'" JUSTIN

"We are making things difficult for ourselves. You get songs like, 'Get Your Hands Off My Woman' and 'Giving Up' – they're potential worldwide super-smash singles and then we go and litter them with swear words." JUSTIN

THE DARKNESS *Talking*

Christmas Time (Don't Let The Bells End)

"A masterpiece – a true work of art that will be around for years to come." DAN

"I just cannot wait for people to hear (the Xmas single). I'm really proud of it actually. It's one of those things that has grown into a monster and when it's finally finished we'll be like 'Oh my God, what have we done?' We'll be playing it every year for the next 20 or 30 years. But what I like about it is the fact it's quite a sad, reflective song, it's got everything that a Christmas song should have… and it *rocks!*" DAN

"Next year we'll be Number 1 at Xmas. But I think this year it's gonna be numero deux. You mark my words." JUSTIN

"Whatever will be will be. I think it will be the one that has the most resonance whether it's number one or not. It's the best song out there. It's the most traditional song of the bunch apart from the (*Pop Idol*) John Lennon cover, which is ludicrous!" JUSTIN

"It's quite a personal song – it was recorded at Abbey Road with Bob Ezrin (producer of Alice Cooper, Pink Floyd, Kiss) – its got a kiddies' choir on, sleigh bells, tubular bells and it's a double A-side with 'Friday Night'!" ED

"Originally, the kids (in the choir on 'Christmas Time') were supposed to sing, 'Bell-end!' really brutally. But the producer complained." ED

"He said, 'bells end and ring in peace, doesn't rhyme'. I said, it doesn't matter – it's bell-end and ring-piece, and all the blood went out of his face. You could see him thinking, you're going to get me fucking sued." JUSTIN

"A few weeks ago it was 66 to 1, then two weeks ago it was 12 to 1, and now it's 4 to 1 – second favourite for Number 1. *Fame Academy* is favourite, and *Bo Selecta* and Westlife are bringing out releases too. We're quite hopeful but we'll definitely be in the Top 5. Because it's got 'Friday Night' as a double A-side and the videos are really good, we're quite optimistic – they're probably the best videos we've done so far!" ED

"'Christmas time, don't let the bells end, just let them ring in peace', that's moving for me. There's no shame in doing a Christmas single. It is a special period of time. I think it gets a bit desperate when you do Mother's Day songs, or Father's Day songs, but Christmas is different." JUSTIN

"I think, once we've given Cliff (Richard) the spanking he deserves in the charts this Christmas, we can safely say that this has been the best year of my life. And when I say 'we', I mean this sweet nation that is the music world." JUSTIN

THE MUSIC

THE DARKNESS Talking

You're Really Growing On Me

"We were aiming for Top 20 in terms of the campaign that we structured, and the nature of that single means that it's not a genuine radio smash, it's a grower ironically, and it ended up at Number 11, then a week later it was still in the Top 20. So we have achieved our goal with that one, the next one is a radio smash."
JUSTIN

"People have said it's about pubic lice. But that's obviously wrong because pubic lice don't grow on you, do they? It's about a sweet lady woman that you will never fully fathom or understand, but you love her so much that after a while it doesn't matter." JUSTIN

Black Shuck

"Justin wrote that song. It's a legend that you hear about when you grow up. It's something that you're aware of at school and everyone talks about it.
"We went on school trips and would look at the old church and the door and see the scratch marks. It's embellished the legend a bit."
DAN

❝I went to Blythburg church again recently and looked at the documents from that fateful day, and none of them actually mention a dog at all. But there was a bloke and a boy that were both killed 'stark dead'. They were killed stark bollock dead, after being electrocuted by lightning. Stabbed by lightning, you might say. I suspect it was some weird gay sex thing and they were killed by lightning during the act and people had to make up this myth to cover up the fact that blokes were shagging in the graveyard.❞ JUSTIN

❝If you take a young creature and remove an eye, or a nostril or a tooth, the other one moves into the middle. That's what I love about nature. It has a way of rectifying itself. The story I heard was that Black Shuck had one eye but, having researched more closely, I discovered that it actually had two eyes. I was *livid!* I felt like I'd been let down by nature. Some of the stuff I've read on the Internet says that Black Shuck didn't even have a head. It just had two eyes. I wonder how that worked? Were they eyes on stalks? You'd expect them to dangle like a pair of bollocks, wouldn't you?❞ JUSTIN

Holding My Own

❝He (Justin) approaches a serious matter in a silly way. It's like 'Holding My Own' is, on the surface, about wanking. But it's also about something deeper than that.❞ ED

B-sides

❝We're not going to put B-sides on the album. We like to put ourselves under pressure – we work better that way, so we put some of our best stuff out as B-sides. We're starting work on songs for our second album already.❞ ED

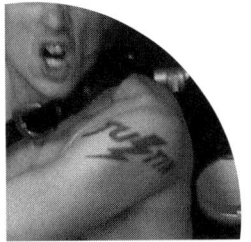

THE MUSIC

THE DARKNESS *Talking*

"B-sides are very important to us – especially now because we've only got one album and we're doing really big shows. We'll be playing stuff from this album for another year, and by then we'll be playing big arenas. So the B-sides need to be as good as the A-sides, or more rockin'..." DAN

"The only time I've thought of death is in terms of doing B-sides, to save them for the next album. But I'm thinking 'Hit by a bus, parting gesture, shit B-side.'" JUSTIN

Permission To Land

"For many moons, we have been bracing ourselves for a shift in the public's perception of The Darkness from underdogs to world-beaters. Our debut album will undoubtedly be a catalyst for this transition. About time, too!" JUSTIN

"**The whole reason we're working so hard and why we've high ambitions for this album is because it's an introduction. We really want this album to be as big as it possibly can be so the next album people will know who we are and we won't have to spend every spare second of every single day working our arses off on it. That light at the end of the tunnel of a couple weeks off at the year after next would be *awesome*.**" DAN

"Before the album, I couldn't even afford to change my strings, much less buy effects pedals." FRANKIE

"There was no room to experiment or relax. We were quite literally working all day, every day." ED

"Generally the stuff we've recorded has tried to get that raw energy back because in a way the single was a little over-produced and lost a little impact. We meandered from the manifesto slightly. A couple of songs from the single are going to be on there because we only pressed a thousand copies of it."
JUSTIN

"It has been all about timing. We could've been signed a couple of years ago and made not nearly as good a record. We had a huge collection of songs and opted to take our time, weed out the great from the not so great, to come up with the ones that are on *Permission To Land*." FRANKIE

"As a debut album *Permission To Land* is up there with the best debut albums ever because it sounds huge, and the songs are brilliant. I'm proud of all of it. There is nothing concept about it, nothing funny, just a proper rocking album." JUSTIN

"I thought 'That Beyoncé, she's a cow!' You can't really be disappointed with Number 2 but it was a relief when it finally went to Number 1 – and for four weeks! We kept Iron Maiden off the top spot. I was really surprised. It was a great thing for us. I anticipate getting assaulted by Bruce Dickinson if ever we meet."
JUSTIN

THE MUSIC

THE DARKNESS *Talking*

"We re-recorded 'Love On The Rocks With No Ice' (for the album)... 'I Believe In A Thing Called Love' was re-mastered and the single again was re-mixed, so the one you hear now on the video is slightly different from the album version. It's got a bigger drum sound on it." ED

"It was going to be like, 'The Darkness request permission to land, they're hungry. Get that fucking Concorde off the runway.' We never did that in the end, so we just kept the title. There were some heavy-duty titles suggested: 'Bad Pennis' was one of them." JUSTIN

"There are some little jokes and puns in there. You can't beat a good pun. Actually, I wanted to call the album 'All Puns Blazing'. Anyway, it's not poodle rock, or pomp rock. I like to call it *luxurious* rock." JUSTIN

"I'm sure I've had every single song on the album as a favourite track since we recorded it. But live at the moment, 'Giving Up' is my favourite, 'cos it's the next single, and because of the chorus words 'Giving up, giving up, giving a fuck...' – there's something amusing about that!" ED

"I particularly like the last two lines of 'Friday Night'. They still move me a lot. And I love the last guitar solo in 'Holding My Own' too. But my favourite song is probably 'Black Shuck'." JUSTIN

"We had a lot of ground to cover, and two weeks to do it in, basically. We just rehearsed the songs as much as we could, and went in and nailed it. I don't think we got a lot of sleep in that fortnight." DAN

"The first song we wrote for the album was probably 'Love On The Rocks With No Ice'. We've been closing the set with it since the beginning of time. We've recorded it three times now: it was on the first EP, there was a demo of it a long time ago and now there's an album version, too. I think we thought it would be a worldwide smash when we wrote it, but it's too long to be a single, isn't it?"
JUSTIN

"We had a set of 50 songs. We thought the album would start with 'Bareback' and that 'Friday Night' and 'Growing On Me' would end up as B-sides. But when we recorded, it became patently obvious what we had to do. It's a good job we recorded those other songs, because we'd never gigged them before and we'd only just written them." JUSTIN

THE DARKNESS ALBUM LAUNCH PARTY IN LONDON

"(Producer Pedro Ferreira) is world class. He's my favourite producer for vocals and I've worked with a grand total of two to date. He's brilliant. He understands rock." JUSTIN

"If I could go and do it all again I probably wouldn't bother. I wouldn't change anything. I think that an album should be a document that states where a band is at, and after that you should just move on. They should be recorded as quickly as possible, like this album was. I like the rawness. It really indicates the poverty that we were enduring and there's something really special about it." JUSTIN

THE MUSIC

THE DARKNESS *Talking*

That 'Difficult' Second Album

"We do work our asses off. There are a few days between shows during Big Day Out, and we're probably the only band on the bill that hasn't had a day off since the start. We squeezed a video shoot in the first two days that we had off, and the last two days we had off we booked ourselves into a studio and started writing and jamming new stuff." DAN

"I hope it's some time this year (2004). We need to write new stuff and finish off the B-sides to this lot of singles too. I don't want it to be five years of solid touring and then finally get round to doing a shit one. I mean, just spend a couple of weeks in the studio and do another one like this, you know, another good 'un." JUSTIN

"We're totally geared up. Apart from world domination our objective is writing the second album. We're writing it already and we've already got a few real gems." DAN

"Labels have to make their investments work, but I think that rather than flogging us like dogs in the short term it would be better for us to make another album as soon as possible. I feel really strongly about that." JUSTIN

"It's one of those things, you've got to strike while the iron is hot and we're pretty creative at the moment. You'd think we'd be completely devoid of ideas, but in the two days we spent in the studio in Melbourne we had eight ideas, four of which are almost completed songs and two of which we're gonna introduce into the live set quite soon. So we're right on course." DAN

"Rome wasn't built in a day. I think our second album is crucial and we're working on that already." JUSTIN

"We want to try and incorporate some larger soundscapes for the next album, but rather than have a piano onstage, I'm going to do a double-neck synthesiser and guitar thing." JUSTIN

"The people who bought *Permission To Land* will be looking forward to the next one, and that's all we have to worry about."
DAN

"It's going to be another big collection of big rock songs. How hard can *that* be? We'll save the jazz concept for the 'difficult' third album." JUSTIN

"Everyone talks about the 'difficult' second album, but the difficulty for us lies only in finding time to record it." JUSTIN

"Once we've made the new album, they won't be disappointed." JUSTIN

THE MUSIC

THE DARKNESS *Talking*

Men On A Mission

"We were always after the big bucks. To sell out as soon as we had a buyer." JUSTIN

"It was our mission to sell out as soon as humanly possible." DAN

"For starters, we're not a joke band, and secondly, there's no reason why you can't be a serious band and have fun at the same time just because everyone else in the last 10 years has been a bunch of miserable bastards." DAN

"I think we're a classic, British rock band with a lot of humour. And that's probably where people have the problem, really, because the current climate is such that having fun is not necessarily the done thing. But it's not going to stop us." JUSTIN

"If you wrote down what the Darkness are and described it to me. I would probably think, 'Oh, that sounds awful.' We have made life hard for ourselves, the way we present things." FRANKIE

"There's nothing else like us around. And that's really sad. What's happened to this nation if we haven't got two decent rock bands? There's no-one anywhere near us." JUSTIN

"In this country signing to a major label would not have made any difference 'cos we've still got the same independent team working with us. The only thing is, we're doing stuff in Germany and America." JUSTIN

"We're on a mission to play the music that we love and have as good a time personally as we can. At the same time playing to as many people as we can. The bigger we get I think the more it's changing things, which is great, but we didn't set out to do that. We just wanted to be as big as we possibly could be." DAN

"We've all been in bands before and the lesson we've learnt is that you have to be yourself, you have to do what you like otherwise what you do is going to be watered down. For our pains we're equally reviled and loved but that's great. People look at us and that's what it's all about." FRANKIE

"When we kicked it off we thought it'd be the hugest thing in the world and everyone would go 'Fucking hell! That's what a band used to sound like and that's how they should sound!' It'd be a fresh new sound for the kids that weren't old enough to have these stadium car-park experiences. We always thought we'd be snapped up by a global conglomerate and pushed in every country in the whole wide world and be the biggest thing on earth 'cos no-one else, at that time, was doing it. But it didn't happen like that, we just got a really strong following. It's only like the last few months that we've really started kicking arse y'know. We were just doing it 'cos we enjoyed it and, if anyone else liked it, it was a bonus! But it wasn't a cynical approach, y'know – we had to rock. We couldn't stop rocking, now everyone else wants to rock as well!" JUSTIN

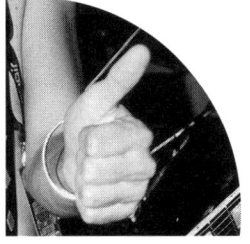

MEN ON A MISSION

THE DARKNESS Talking

"Everyone's too uptight these days. I hate the arrogance of bands who think their petty emotions are interesting. If you look at bands from 25 years ago, people have smiles on their faces. We're bringing a bit of that back." **FRANKIE**

"We're well aware that some people are waiting for the backlash. Many want it to start tomorrow. But all we're doing is bringing people together and showing them a good time." ED

"The people that don't like our music are people I wouldn't want to know or be friends with anyway. You just can tell the people who are cynically unable to get into it, and people that are just basically tired of life." **DAN**

"It's like the three stages of rabies. First people fear us, then they start foaming at the mouth because they want us. And then they start attacking other people." JUSTIN

"We don't do generic music." **FRANKIE**

"People making *Spinal Tap* comparisons don't know what we're about. We're not some made-up band. We write our own songs. We perform our own songs." JUSTIN

"With today's music, it's cool to complain and feel sorry for yourself. I can't stand it. I want to have a good time when I listen to music." **FRANKIE**

"There are bands that are all icing and no cake. We are the cake that gives you icing." DAN

"And we're not cheesecake either." **ED**

"Dan likes everything to be perfect. He's had a lot of techs working for him because he's done a lot of session work in the past. Probably the worst thing that happened was his Line 6 pedal going down at the Astoria. It's a big part of his sound and his solos and it just stopped working for some season. We have a backstage workshop made out of a flight case with a tool case on top of it for things like that." RICK STACY (DAN'S GUITAR TECH)

"No-one saw this one coming, did they? Even the label that signed us thought we'd do well to sell 60,000 albums by Christmas, and we did that in the second week. No-one was told that we were the best thing since sliced egg, they just bought the album because they thought we were good. It's a good indication that people are getting sick of being told what to buy. We're not a Pepsi Challenge band. We're a real, organic organisation with good people around us. It's encouraging for other bands like us, hopefully." JUSTIN

"I think people find it hard to believe what they're actually seeing. They think there's some kind of ironic masterplan behind it but there isn't. We're just doing what we really like doing." DAN

"(Atlantic/East West) were the company that agreed to take on the team that were working for us, often for free, up to the point of us getting a record deal. We sold out without selling out." JUSTIN

"We were too big to win the (2003) Mercury Music Prize."
DAN

"I don't feel we should ram this thing down people's throats and that's my vibe. I'll do 365 gigs a year – I'm not lazy in that way – and I will deliver on promises and commitments." JUSTIN

MEN ON A MISSION

Friends & NMEs

"The editor of the *New Musical Express* calls me up and I keep telling him to 'fuck off', but then he called our press bloke and said that was the most rock'n'roll thing that had ever happened to him. You wouldn't think the *NME* would sell their readers short by putting a band on the cover without an interview. We're boycotting them. They have no chance with any of us ever co-operating with them. I don't care if we're cutting off our noses to spite our faces, I'd rather not have a face at all. They're a bunch of inadequate journalists that know nothing. This is war." JUSTIN

"The Darkness were really, really inoffensive. I don't know why people hate them or like them. It doesn't do anything for me. I'm not sure if the people who like them do genuinely like them."
NOEL GALLAGHER

"Scepticism – it's a British disease." FRANKIE

THE DARKNESS *Talking*

"The Darkness make me happy. That cat Justin Hawkins loves to rock, and the people love him." JANE'S ADDICTION SINGER PERRY FARRELL

"There have been sour grapes from a few people in the industry as well. One particular individual, a veteran rocker, was very bitter about us at the *Kerrang!* awards this year for stealing the show. But things have to change." FRANKIE

"Mick Jagger just popped his head round the corner and said 'All right?', then Keith Richards came in with his eyes wobbling, living it, really living the dream, you know – still doing it." JUSTIN

"The Prime Minister, Tony Blair, likes us. It was in the paper." JUSTIN

"I'd love to meet U2. I think Bono could give us some good advice." FRANKIE

"Actually I'm a bit nervous about Metallica, because what we stand for is what they were fighting against – guitar solos, flamboyancy and big hair. And now their new album has gone back to those old ethics – no solos, no bullshit. Apparently though, Lars Ulrich has been bigging us up and saying that he likes us... but that doesn't always extend to the crowd." JUSTIN

"Mick (Jagger) came up to us and it was like 'Hello boys!' And then Keith (Richards) was like, 'Oh, there's some good old flames on that one...'"
JUSTIN (WHO HAS A TATTOO OF FLAMES ON HIS BELLY) ON SUPPORTING THE STONES

"'How 'bout them Darkness guys? It's like the old days, isn't it?'"
US CHAT-SHOW HOST DAVID LETTERMAN

"Generally you have to ignore anything *NME* writes about us. Recently I met the editor of *NME* and he said to me 'You are going to hate me when I tell you who I am', so I said 'Who are you?' and he replied 'I'm the editor of *NME*' to which I said 'Well fuck off then!' because they slagged us off in the early days and we don't do features with them, we don't do anything with them. So they like to have a little dig here and there, but *Kerrang!* have looked after us since the beginning so we are nice to them. *Kerrang!* have got it right, but *NME* are not going to be accurate." JUSTIN

"I like the single, it's a catchy song, but it's not metal. It's pop-rock. How dare they call themselves metal? That's not metal. It'll never be metal!
"Don't claim to be something you're not. Don't claim to be metal. Don't claim that you're authentic and we're not. Fuck you!"
DAVID DRAIMAN, FRONTMAN OF HEAVY METAL OUTFIT DISTURBED

"Def Leppard have been great to open for, and so have The Wildhearts. We don't assume that, having played with these people, we're instantly innovated to their status. The minute you start getting arrogant about that, is when you stop making friends. We can't afford to do that just yet. When we headline, then we'll become *real* arseholes!" JUSTIN

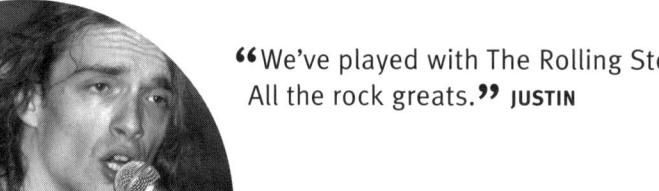

"We've played with The Rolling Stones and Meatloaf. All the rock greats." JUSTIN

FRIENDS & NMEs

THE DARKNESS *Talking*

"We're such boring, cynical stiffs in this country, aren't we? We don't know how to handle showmanship. I love all that stuff and The Darkness do it so well. It's a shame that people have to be so cynical about it." RADIO 1 DJ JO WHILEY

"When I actually saw their video I wasn't too sure because it seemed like a piss-take and a bit fake, but then I saw them play at Download and I realised how good they were. They've built up a real head of steam over here, so they've got a great chance of doing well internationally. That's great news for British rock music. They kept Maiden off the Number 1 spot, but we'd rather lose to a real rock band than anyone else."

IRON MAIDEN MANAGER ROD SMALLWOOD

"They're fun, aren't they? I was talking to Brian May about them because they're closer to his home than mine. I think, yeah, they're good. It's fun, there's a sense of humour to it, but there's a lot of good playing going on there, good riffs." LED ZEPPELIN'S JIMMY PAGE

"*NME* criticised us when we weren't successful. Now we're the biggest band in England and these shits are making fools of themselves by trying to kiss our behinds." DAN

"The Darkness are my favourite band right now. I've had that sensibility for ages, so it was a great relief when they came out. I've just had to do an inventory of my costumes because I'm donating them to the Museum of Performing Arts in Australia, and some of the descriptions would be appreciated by The Darkness. Like 'Red leather hot-pant minirumper with lace-up corset and hand-painted sheer bat wings!'" KYLIE MINOGUE

"There was the odd sniper in the British press. We weren't doing so well and writers would come out saying, 'There's something not right about this. It's put together.' It was suspicion for what we were doing. This sort of rock scene has been uncool for so long due to movies like *Wayne's World* and *Spinal Tap*, people wondered how we could be serious about it." FRANKIE

"I've known the band for a few years through (drummer) Ed Graham and I asked them on the last tour if they needed a hand."
RICK STACY (DAN'S GUITAR TECH)

"My brother has a theory that anyone who wears capes is cool. Like Justin from The Darkness, Superman, Elvis, Liberace and James Brown." KYLIE MINOGUE

"'Fuckin' weird cunts! Show me what you can do without a 20-foot fuckin' vegetable running around behind you!'"
FRANKIE QUOTING NOEL GALLAGHER ON THEIR '...THING CALLED LOVE' VIDEO

"There is a weekly magazine that we've quite happily boycotted. We've made a lot of friends by doing that. We don't dance with people that stand on our toes, because otherwise you end up with clown-feet. And then people call you, 'Penguin-boy'. Stuff that!"
JUSTIN

FRIENDS & NMEs

THE DARKNESS *Talking*

"Oasis must have strutted in (to America), four and a half foot tall or whatever they are, thinking, 'Oh God, this country's ours for the taking!' and then as soon as it doesn't go their way they go, 'Ooh, that's not quite working, is it? Shall we go back to the UK where we're really popular and successful?' Knock it on the head, can't be bothered with this. To me, it's laziness and arrogance. I'm not really sure how good they are, either." JUSTIN

"Yesterday I was walking down Belsize Park with Justin and our manager Sue when this huge people carrier with blacked-out windows stops before us. Liam Gallagher emerged, shuffled up to us in his monkey walk and said 'Top band! Top band!' There was a moment's pause and then he just shuffled back into his van. It was a nice moment, a moment – how would I describe it? – like when Proust on his *Remembrance Of Things Past,* he dipped his teacake in his hot beverage and that reminded him of his childhood. Liam Gallagher was the teacake." FRANKIE

LIAM GALLAGHER

"*Kerrang!* built us up and they're perfectly within their rights to knock us down now. They've given us everything they can give us and been really supportive whereas the *NME* have just knocked us down. In a way their love is more intense, it's more about a humanistic passion for us as people rather than the music. They know that we're newsworthy, really, but they're idea is that if they can't have us then no-one can have us. They'd rather destroy us than let someone else... bed us!" JUSTIN

62

"The South by Southwest show went really well. There was loads of industry (people) there, British and American; all the music companies were buying us steak in the best places. They took us to one of the most expensive restaurants in town and would buy us steak and lobster that cost sixty dollars a plate. It was like a double-decker. And then we came back and the *NME* says 'The Darkness, like Ali G, came to America and America saw through the bullshit.' Which means that either they didn't go to the show or they went to the show and decided to lie about it. If someone doesn't like you they don't like you, but just to write lies all the time just to slate you is really offensive." ED

"Liam Gallagher came up to me the other day outside a restaurant in Belsize Park. He jumped out of his car and came to say hello and it really moved me in a way, because he's the most famous person in rock." JUSTIN

"(Style mag *Dazed And Confused*'s) angle was 'This is a real band, they're real fucking losers, but they still plug away and drive to Wolverhampton to play to five people.' It wasn't actually the rock that was fashionable about that piece. At the time the angle was 'What a bunch of losers!' Uncool. Uncool is the new cool. These are the real ones, the ones that try really hard but never get anywhere.' It was ironic. The coverage was nice, don't get me wrong, it was a boost for our perception." JUSTIN

"People have misconceptions. All this stuff about style mags being interested in us, it was our one and only piece and it wasn't even a fashion piece." FRANKIE

"We're brilliant. We're making rock fun. We're not boring like Coldplay, we don't take ourselves that seriously but we're still flying the flag for Britain. We get great responses from everyone, from the public to people like Robbie Williams, Tom Jones. Even (ex-BBC Royal reporter) Jennie Bond likes us." JUSTIN

FRIENDS & NMEs

THE DARKNESS *Talking*

"Secretly the (critics) don't know what they're hating. That kind of hate can turn to love. It's the same as when you're with a lady, like the Clark Gable kind of movies where the woman hits him but she really loves him. The *NME* will sleep with us eventually. They'll probably have to do it against our will, they'll probably have to rape us!" FRANKIE

"We're real people and we're a band that's been playing on the scene for a long time. We've made a lot of friends and one enemy we've always had was the *NME*. They've always slated us and they've basically never ever written about the music. They've just said that we should be hung for crimes against music and while never once describing about what we're actually about. Suddenly they put us on the front cover of the *NME* to sell more magazines because they're a really awful magazine, but as soon as they're done with us and we're off the scene they'll start slagging us off again. One thing we can say is that we've never spoken to them, *ever*." DAN

"I think there's fewer good bands coming out of Britain than there has been in years. I don't know whether it's post Brit-pop, but it must be post nu-metal now as well and working out where it's trying to go. But the kids are still kind of buying guitar music blindly!" JUSTIN

"I think we're an improvement on sliced bread!"

"I can confirm that there is nothing freakish about my genitalia."

"It was our mission to sell out as soon as humanly possible."

"Are we the gay AC/DC? I prefer the straight Queen!"

What D'ya Think?

"Daniel Bedingfield's got a lovely voice. He's definitely talented." DAN

"I think 'If You're Not The One' was a brilliantly penned and performed ballad. The rest of it I don't know, I'm not really sure about it." JUSTIN

"Most of these modern bands are so unbearably serious they leave me cold. Radiohead are totally boring. The world needs a showman like Justin who puts on his monkey outfit and entertains people. I haven't bought anything by these modern bands in a while. They're all wet rags. Bands like Radiohead are great for our business, of course, because there's been a total Radiohead-isation of the British music scene. Coldplay, Turin Brakes, Starsailor – all of these groups have put together their selection from the Radiohead menu." DAN

"We really enjoyed touring with Def Leppard, Ten Benson and The Wildhearts – they were the three best ones. I would like to tour with Aerosmith because I think we would do really well. Also the big challenge would be AC/DC, but that would just be a piss-dodging exercise, as their fans are really hard to please." JUSTIN

"If I was waiting to see AC/DC, I wouldn't give a fuck how good they were on the day – I'd still be trying to bottle them off!" DAN

WHAT D'YA THINK?

THE DARKNESS *Talking*

"Certain areas of the cool press revere him as a guitar player, but he's an idiot. And he's got an Epiphone signature guitar."
JUSTIN ON NOEL GALLAGHER

"Bands like Kiss and Poison over-iced the cake, they had no real backbone, whereas AC/DC and Queen and a lot of classic British rock bands really had that showmanship, too." JUSTIN

GENE SIMMONS OF KISS

"We're probably a bigger band than Def Leppard in the UK now, but when they play they've got this thing about playing arenas instead of playing in front of two thousand people or so. They sound better and look better as a result – and it's just *awesome*. It's good watching how they go about it and what they do, and from the way they approach these gigs we learned a lot from that, more than from any of the other bands we played with." DAN

"Are we the gay AC/DC? I prefer the straight Queen!" JUSTIN

"I don't like Bon Jovi because they're so corporate. You go see them now and it's fucking *Ally McBeal* music. He's had his teeth changed and his hair cut and looks like a cunt." JUSTIN

"Is Jamie Cullum the jazz piano player who was signed for an awful lot of money to EMI? He was talking about covering one of our songs at one point. He was going to do 'I Believe In A Thing Called Love' but in the piano style, which would be interesting." JUSTIN

"I met Dido and she's one of those people that everyone thinks is from... I actually said to her, 'You're from Ipswich, aren't you?' And apparently people think she's from Tunbridge Wells. But she's actually from Islington. I've sat down and had a meal with her and I think she's very charming and intelligent, and unusually bright lady. I wish her all the best. I won't hear a bad word against her, even though she scuppered our chances of being at Number 1 for five weeks." JUSTIN

"Beyoncé? In a word, awesome. Very talented in many ways." DAN

"Sweet lady. Nice dancing and good singing, I like her."
FRANKIE ON BEYONCÉ

"She's got balls!" JUSTIN ON BEYONCÉ

"Christina Aguilera's dirty but her music's all right!" ED

"I like her because she's feisty. She's a kind of pop version of Courtney Love. I think she's shifted the goalpost; she's got a lot to be congratulated for." DAN ON CHRISTINA AGUILERA

"I think it's silly wearing leather pants *that* small. She's got a nice voice but some of those outfits, you know... I don't buy it. I don't think she's anywhere near as dirty as she makes out. I think she's double posh." JUSTIN ON CHRISTINA AGUILERA

"We met Busted the other day at a pop show. Yeah, nice lads. Fairly loud, they wear Darkness T-shirts, obviously got good taste, nice guys." DAN

"I was never really a huge Iron Maiden fan but I recognise the significance that they hold. In a way I felt quite bad about keeping them off the top spot when their album came out this year, because at that time we were kind of looking to do some stuff with them. They're middle-aged rockers but they deserve to be where they are." JUSTIN

WHAT D'YA THINK?

THE DARKNESS *Talking*

"Maiden are still around – it's good for music that they are because they're rock legends." **DAN**

"We're going to be Number 2 and Beyoncé's going to be Number 1. Underneath Beyoncé's not a bad place to be, if you know what I mean." **JUSTIN**

"I hope to meet Robbie (Williams), he seems like a really nice bloke. A lot of his stuff is a send-up and that's maybe something we didn't really want to be associated with, but you can't turn down a crowd that big." **JUSTIN ON BEING SUPPORT ACT AT KNEBWORTH**

"Queen used to be something worth fighting for, but I think Brian May has butchered the back catalogue and allowed fucking people like Five to ruin the memory." **JUSTIN**

"I've been sparring and riffing with other bands. I was saying hello to Kirk from Metallica, the guys from Flaming Lips, The Black Eyed Peas. They're all brilliant people." **JUSTIN**

"I was really looking forward to meeting the Flaming Lips because us and them got slagged off by Noel Gallagher in the UK press." **JUSTIN**

"Noel Gallagher is an overrated guitarist losing grip on his credibility who just has to fire desperate shots on his way down. It's kind of a shame, really." **JUSTIN**

The Brits

"This is the award we all secretly hoped for – it's *huge*."
JUSTIN ACCEPTING BEST BRITISH ALBUM

"We should thank our parents for bestowing the greatness of rock on us. It's the gift that keeps on giving." **JUSTIN**

"Well, he is right there, really. He was brought up from the age of two listening to rock." **MRS HAWKINS**

"This is a real privilege, a tremendous honour and a great achievement. I have to say we probably *are* the best British group." **JUSTIN**

"We're absolutely chuffed that we are nominated for four awards and are looking forward to the big night. Hopefully this will help us towards getting our MBEs for services to rock." **DAN**

"We're going to win easily. There is no way we are going to miss out on these awards." **JUSTIN**

"We're going to do something different because we can. We're going to make sure the Darkness totally rock the Brits." **JUSTIN**

"We weren't invited to the Brits last year, we were on tour supporting Def Leppard which was brilliant. This has been a truly amazing year for us but we think there is a lot better to come."
JUSTIN

THE BRITS

THE DARKNESS *Talking*

"We're planning something very, very special (For the Brits). Everyone will have to wait and see." FRANKIE

"I anticipate we'll win something, you know, based on the fact that we're top of the UK music tree, and nobody can really deny that. Especially not in the rock realms." JUSTIN

"Apparently, they created this category especially for us and we are honoured and privileged."
JUSTIN ON WINNING BEST BRITISH ROCK ACT AWARD

"It's wonderful – wow! My heart is in my throat. The fun's back in music. It couldn't happen to a better bunch of guys. The local paper kindly supplied two bottles of champagne and we are working through it!" SANDY HAWKINS

"Goldilocks In Chains from Newport should be given an award for services to hip-hop. Their record is only available in four shops and this country should get behind them because they know what they're doing. They're class. Ten Benson should be on the rock list as well.

"I really think The Wildhearts should be acknowledged as well, because they're ever present and they're releasing new stuff all the time. And they're moving forward, but they're just not getting the attention they deserve." DAN

"Young Heart Attack should win if there's an international award for being the best band in America." JUSTIN

"It's great to be here but it isn't exactly a surprise – we're definitely the best band here at the show."
JUSTIN ON BEING VOTED BEST BRITISH BAND

"They were trying to give us that Moët and fucking Chandon crap; we don't pour anything less than Cristal." DAN

"I just want to let those wankers at *NME* know that we don't bother with Mickey Mouse ceremonies like the Brats – we just do the real thing. People who slagged us off at the beginning missed the boat and it's too late. I had the editor of the *NME* begging me on his bended knee at Glastonbury but I told him to fuck off! I always knew one day we'd perform at the Brits. If I didn't think that I'd have given up a long time ago. But the big thing is how quickly it's happened. It all kicked off in about 12 months but we've been together for years and years." JUSTIN

SANDY HAWKINS – JUSTIN & DAN'S MUM

"We wanted to do something that would really get people in the spirit. We knew we wanted unicorns and then it sort of went into this Atlantis, underwater theme – the best bit is when I go up into the air on this sixty-foot sparkling silver column. It's very sexual. I feel amazing up there, playing my guitar over the heads of the whole record industry and there I am on this huge erection. **Pure genius.**" JUSTIN

THE BRITS

THE DARKNESS Talking

"I like (fellow Brit Award Winners) Duran Duran. A lot of Eighties stuff was produced in such a way that made it sound very dated very instantly and theirs (Duran Duran) has transcended that sort of decade barrier. I think that track 'Save A Prayer' is a beautiful song. It's a lush piece of music. It's still vital and valid now, isn't it?" JUSTIN

"Yeah, well, we all like Duran Duran, don't we? And apparently they speak very highly of us as well, which is an advantage. They're proper musicians, and they've stood the test of time. We still need to do a video like 'Rio', don't we?" DAN

"Everyone's knackered, we flew back from our European tour yesterday, and we've spent all today at the Brits rehearsals, which is a bit nerve wracking. What are we doing for it? Well, we don't want to give too much away. We'll just get up there and rock out I s'pose, although we have got quite an interesting stage set that will leave a few people scratching their heads – it certainly left me scratching my head when I saw it.

"It's gonna be fun, though. It's a really important thing and we're gonna be enjoying the whole thing as much as we can." DAN

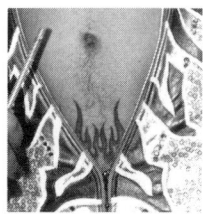

Sex, Drugs, Rock'n'roll

"I've just had a PO Box set up which is called Justin Hawkins' Casual Sex Enquiries, PO Box 69, Lowestoft." JUSTIN

"Dan's girlfriend isn't a model, and of course she's not a groupie. We do have the Darkness Official Groupies, known as the DOGs they're starting to build up quite an organisation. Do they come to all our gigs? Well, they pop up every now and then!" FRANKIE

"Everything is cool in my mind and with how it's going. But you know, the way that my life is at the moment, you've just got to take it one day at a time."
JUSTIN ON HIS NEW LOVE, SINGER JENNIFER STEPHENS FROM US ROCK BAND YOUNG HEART ATTACK

"We got in a dodgy situation the other day with a troop of girl-guides going on a ferry to Holland. On the way back, because of the intensity of that experience, we had to upgrade to club-class on the ferry, absolutely pissed out of our heads and being a total disgrace. Throwing peanuts at the waiters." ED

"I'm looking forward to the Reading Festival because I used to go there all the time, five years on the trot. Until my liver couldn't take any more. We (me and Ed) used to run the fun centre at Reading; it was a few tents in the camp site with 'fun centre' written over it. We had loads of white cider and power-drinking events. A bit like a drinking exhibition. We are looking forward to playing there!"
JUSTIN

SEX, DRUGS, ROCK'N'ROLL

THE DARKNESS *Talking*

"The flamboyant rock revolution, or whatever they're going to call it, we will have spearheaded that in a way. We have been doing this for years. You should see the energy we put into our drinking as well!" JUSTIN

"We've learned to be less self-indulgent. We were guilty of the early AC/DC kind of playing: all excess." JUSTIN

"It is a struggle being on the road. My friends and family worry about me but I'm getting myself together this year (2004)." JUSTIN

"This year has been an *anus memorabilias*. That's Latin for 'memorable arse'. People have chosen the path of rock. I really want to stress this whole anus thing. Every year is a good year for rock, but this *anus memorabilias* has been better than what we could have imagined. And when I say 'we', I mean the universal brotherhood that is rock." JUSTIN

"The difference with rock is that it's all about working hard, playing hard and showing discipline. Indie bands don't have the ability to do any of that." FRANKIE

"Normally, we'd have to go into the studio and do a rush job. But we ended up having to cancel a day in the studio because we're so gig-fit. We've done so many shows we're really ready to rock." JUSTIN

"Women stuff, there's a lot of things explored there. Boobies, bums, drugs. Big dogs with one eye. We can write about anything, really. Sometimes it's nice to be purely erotic, think from the groin occasionally. It's primal, harks back to the glory years when you didn't really need to do anything other than grunt and carry women to your cave. It's always nice to keep in touch with that aspect of it." JUSTIN

"I never slap (my bass). I'm probably the least funky man on the face of the earth." FRANKIE

"Would you rather be on stage or have fantastic sex? I'd rather be on stage *having* fantastic sex." JUSTIN

"We don't really meticulously plan things, we just try to be spontaneous. When we were in America a magazine gave us $848 to spend in four hours on a night out. We were thinking that generally bands go out and get strippers or champagne or drugs, being total arseholes and wasting all the money. We hired a donkey and walked it around New York, given it was New York fashion week and all..." DAN

"The highlight for me was appearing on the cover of *Kerrang!* not once, but twice. That first cover was a real memorable moment for me and I was especially pleased that it was me and not the rest of the band. At that point I thought we had no right to be on the cover – but then we went to Number 1." JUSTIN

SEX, DRUGS, ROCK'N'ROLL

Strutting Their Stuff

"We'll be headlining arenas by next year. They can't wait, it's going to be fucking Beatlemania." JUSTIN

"I like people who respect their instruments and have played the same guitar for years and years. People like Brian May. I think anybody who smashes a guitar up has a problem... why take it out on a beautiful instrument that thousands of people would love to own? It's like writing off a Porsche for the sake of it."
JUSTIN

"This year at Reading was basically a stepping stone to headlining next year. We had the condition that kids who bought day tickets to see us could swap days." JUSTIN

"The singer (of Staind) said to me 'I don't know what you're doing? When people come to a Staind show, they weep at my lyrics.' At the Reading Festival they were in a slot just before us, which is not an easy job. And they struggled. People weren't weeping. They were going, 'Darkness! Darkness!'" JUSTIN

"The point is we strive to make our performances all-encompassing, fun events that work on different sensory levels. It's bombastic, it's showy, but beyond that there's class songs – well-written songs. That was always our plan: to have a product, a catalogue, a repertoire that we're very proud of." JUSTIN

STRUTTING THEIR STUFF

THE DARKNESS *Talking*

"We once talked about rolling around on the stage in a giant hamster ball. If we could pull it off it would be great." DAN

"I think our roadies are just fabulous. They've become part of the show. The professionals look at them and say 'Oh, you wanna look at your guitar techs, they're too conspicuous.' We think there's a lot of things that happen behind the scenes that should happen in front of the scenes." JUSTIN

"We were still an unsigned band but found ourselves headlining the Astoria, so decided as well as three costume changes (that) we needed to get pyros and stuff, and fast. Unfortunately it's very expensive and you need a licence, so the compromise was confetti canons. There were supposed to be eight going off at the same time. Well, two of them went off fine, but the one in front of me just went ppllbb!! The bouncer was looking round at it. We don't go looking for *Spinal Tap* comparisons, but when stuff like this happens it doesn't help does it?" JUSTIN

"I'm the masseur as well – I give the guys massages when they've been head-banging too much. Dan also gives a team talk before they go on stage, which I used to be involved in before my job got too hectic!" TOM JENNINGS (JUSTIN'S TECH)

"I was thinking of having a workbench on stage with a full set of carpentry tools... saws, hammers, drills, things like that. That way I could combine two fine areas of craftsmanship – carpentry and guitar-playing. That would make Bon Jovi look *really* stupid." JUSTIN

"Playing the (London) Astoria was a turning point. We were unsigned and we sold out and it's quite a big venue. There aren't many bands in the world who can say they did that. The nearest equivalent is Omar, who sold out Brixton Academy as an unsigned artist." JUSTIN

"Showmanship is one of the main things that we hold dear. The emphasis is on having a good time and being a multi-sensory experience rather than four blokes just playing their guitar. It is a visual thing, and it's a smell thing, and a touch thing in some cases. It is more of an event than a gig." JUSTIN

"There's a minimum you have to fulfil, otherwise it's just a lead break. It's the time it takes for your shirt to get to maximum openness. A strange thing happens when you're soloing; your balls get bigger and your shirt gets more… opener." JUSTIN

"You know a guitar solo's going well when you swap guitars in the middle and carry on." DAN

"Since day-one, we've always considered ourselves a stadium band. That played in pubs. Or clubs. But, now, it's turned around – we're a pub band playing stadiums." JUSTIN

"A lot of people thought it was a joke at the beginning and the great thing about Manchester was that as soon as the support band finished everyone moved right to the front. For us that is an out-of-town gig and it's a great feeling because it means that people know what they've let themselves in for – it's not just a joke!" JUSTIN

JUSTIN WITH PINK

"The stage show can be really outrageous because the songs are good. You can prance around like an idiot and headbang as much as you like because the song is good. There are lots of bands around that are really into the rocking side of it, they look great and are obviously enjoying themselves, but they haven't got the songs." DAN

STRUTTING THEIR STUFF

THE DARKNESS *Talking*

"In the olden days, everyone used to say, 'You're too big for this pub.' And when you look at videos of us playing in those smaller venues, it looks like we're caged animals trying to get off the stage because we didn't have enough room to manoeuvre. But then the actual time we took the step up and the first couple of shows we actually struggled, like we were trying to do too much with the space.

"But having watched Def Leppard and seeing how they manoeuvre in order to have a presence as a unit was a real eye-opener, and by the end of the tour I think we were giving Leppard a run for their money. Obviously nowadays we're the best in the business at that because we've had so much experience. In the olden days we were ambitious, but now we're accomplished." JUSTIN

"We've served our apprenticeships for these big heavyweight rock bands, and now we're moving onto our own headline tour. We'll be bringing in the pyros next year..." ED

"You could put us in any venue, any size and we'll kick ass. We've played to 125,000 people one day and 100 people two weeks later in Germany. The bigger the stage gets, the more natural it is for us. The roof could cave in on a venue, and we'd still be playing. Ed fell off the back of the stage once and we kept playing." JUSTIN

"We've played nearly every festival going this year (2003) – next year we won't be doing that. We'll be doing more stuff in America and hopefully headline a big festival. We might play two or three, and that'll be it for us in the UK for a while." DAN

"We've done a couple of acoustic gigs, actually – three, in total. They were quite good." FRANKIE

"One thing that was nice about performing that way is that the songs came across even more, and people remarked about them. They could be sung by anyone, and they'd sound great. But the thing is... we're a rock band, that's what we do. I wouldn't mind experimenting with some more medieval, ominous folk-rock, though." DAN

"A band of our ilk is genetically determined to achieve the honour of performing at Knobwerth. It's in our DNA. We've waited years for this opportunity and we're truly grateful and honoured to have been invited! Treading those hallowed boards will have as much emotional impact for me as stepping out on to the pitch at St James' Park has for a Geordie soccer enthusiast." JUSTIN

"As far as the live shows go we're not leapfrogging all the smaller venues. I mean the (London Hammersmith) Apollo, it is a big venue but it is still a lot smaller than what we could be playing right now. We would have bypassed these kind of shows and gone straight to arena shows, but we didn't want to. Although it is a very fast progression, it is a very natural one." DAN

"Just from gigging a lot, we've adapted to larger stages. In the olden days, we'd play in clubs where we had no option but to stand reasonably still because there was so little room; Frankie and Dan would just try and keep out of my way when I was running around. But, now, we've all got a greater understanding of what the other one is up to and command our space a bit more..." JUSTIN

"I'm in the back, supporting Justin." FRANKIE

"We've always behaved like stadium rockers, even at the beginning when we were playing in pubs. This (Wembley Arena) is our manor." JUSTIN

STRUTTING THEIR STUFF

THE DARKNESS *Talking*

"We're going to have the Arse de Triomphe, a huge fibreglass bottom that opens up and we walk through onto the stage. I've always fancied flying over the crowd with a jet pack." JUSTIN

"We've not even been into a rehearsal room. We didn't even have time to have a rehearsal before Knebworth (where they supported Robbie Williams). It was like 'Fucking hell, we're playing to 375,000 people and we hadn't even had a rehearsal.'"
ED

"We're first on the bill at Knebworth and every other poor bastard will have to live up to our performance. We try to make it a spectacle. It's a different set of values to what some of the other bands have." JUSTIN

"The crowds at our gigs now tend to be half nerds and half supermodels. They'll soon start breeding kids who are hyper-intelligent, very self-conscious but gorgeous with really long legs." FRANKIE

"If you're playing in front of a camera crew, sometimes they have these microphones that operate on the same frequency as our transmitter systems. We had a TV programme come and film us, and throughout the gig the bass cut in and out whenever they turned their microphone on or off. It was just like that *Spinal Tap* moment on the military base. Meanwhile the presenter's commentary was coming out of the bass amp!"
JUSTIN

"I feel now its really exciting. All the stuff that we're doing is what the kids have been scrabbling for a while now. Stadium rock. Or cock rock. Or whatever you want to call it." JUSTIN

"Well within three weeks of playing with Robbie we supported Metallica in Dublin to 45,000 people and both gigs went off as nuts as each other. The kids and the oldies at the Robbie gig were getting into it and boogieing on down and going 'Oh, look at these young men rocking' and then we go to Dublin and play with Metallica and everyone just goes absolutely mental. There's not many bands like that. We're not a niche band at all." DAN

"I am working on a new signature move – I've had a few in the past. In one, I do a solo and finish on an open string, but the flourish is I lean back and put both my thumbs up: instant crowd reaction. Another one is, I do a solo and then, while trilling with one hand, the other hand comes up behind the head and then you use your fingers to make a fringe while still widdling. You know. It's a symmetry thing. And it's to do with thought processes and motions and...it never actually caught on." JUSTIN

STRUTTING THEIR STUFF

Lights, Camera, Action

Video for 'I Believe In A Thing Called Love'

"We've had one (giant squid) in our videos. We come up with these mad ideas and then our poor director has to make it happen." DAN

"Call him (director) up and say, 'We'd like a giant crab, please', and he goes and makes us one." ED

Video for 'Get Your Hands Off My Woman'

"Everything's going swimmingly, and I'm terribly excited by it all. I've seen a rough cut of the video, and it looks like a gig, which is mission accomplished, I think. We're hoping to have a screening somewhere – a grand occasion with a lovely buffet and prawn sandwiches for the elite and what have you. I substituted the word coconut for cunt, and motherfucker became mummamumma, just mumbled into obscurity. It scans well, so we're all right." JUSTIN

Video for 'Christmas Time (Don't Let The Bells End')

"The video is a mix of every Christmas video you've ever seen in your life. The kids are wearing bobble hats, scarves and mittens

THE DARKNESS Talking

tied together with string so they don't lose them on a cold winter's night. We thought about getting some elves. But we couldn't get any real ones, so we offered a load of midgets who would have worn big ears." JUSTIN

Video for 'You're Really Growing On Me'

"When we did 'Growing On Me', we just had Alex (Smith) with his little camera and the budget was minuscule. He basically worked his ass off to make it happen – I don't think he even paid himself." JUSTIN

"This time Alex (Smith) managed to assemble a whole team of people: cameramen, runners, health and safety officers, producers and set builders. It was a really amazing experience, 'cos there were like 20 or 30 people on set pandering to our every request. Fabulous experience – that's why we're in this game." JUSTIN

Video 'Love Is Only A Feeling'

"What would you rather do? Sit on a beach and get sunburnt or run around on a cliff with a guitar chasing a helicopter?" DAN

"There are helicopters circling around mountain tops... ya know, it was kind of taking the Darkness, the album, to its natural conclusion, and we really wanted to go out with a bang. We hadn't really done a performance video before. We've covered a lot of angles, and this was our chance to show people that we are capable of being the huge rock gods that everyone wants us to be. What we're actually doing is the outrageous side of it. Put it this way, there won't be any sort of firefly monsters or giant squids or crabs walking around. It's gonna look huge!" DAN

"The record company's plan is to shoot something very big-budget, really glamorous-looking." FRANKIE

"The record company wants us to do the whole mountain/guitars/helicopter thing." DAN

Catsuits & Lipstick

"If you go and see a stadium band that wears grey clothes and looks at their shoes, are you going to enjoy that as much as a band that has pyrotechnics and a bloke leaping around like Aerosmith? I think that's what makes my favourite bands better than other people's favourite bands. It's something that sets them apart." JUSTIN

"I've had my moustache since I was born, it's called nappy tash. It just grows naturally..." FRANKIE

"Mick Jagger liked my velvet loons, but I don't think he could really be bothered with the 30 minutes it takes to get into them – and then you have to allow that again every time you need to go to the toilet." JUSTIN

"I never wear pants with my catsuits, it's a commando job. You can't have any VPL. It's not a good look." JUSTIN

"I think I'm the voice of reason. But we're all different people. I don't like some of the poses in photos, so I won't do them any more. And I don't like flares. I won't wear them." ED

CATSUITS & LIPSTICK

THE DARKNESS *Talking*

"We want to be playing really big venues and we want to able to connect and you have to be able do that visually as well as sonically. It's an important aspect of it." JUSTIN

"I find those twins (from TV's 118 118 adverts) with the moustaches a bit dispiriting. It's really naff. I came out before them, anyway." FRANKIE

"I contacted a dance studio that made rehearsal uniforms and they custom-made something for me. But they'd just stuck together some cheap Lycra and my balls were hanging out everywhere. They gave me a jockstrap that was flesh-coloured to try to keep it all in but it just didn't cut it." JUSTIN

"Once I had to be cut out of my trousers because they got stuck to me while I was on stage. Then there was the time we were on a TV show in Ireland. I did a big jump and I split my pants – you could see everything! I don't think we'll be asked back." JUSTIN

"This feather (in the lapel of the crushed velvet suit jacket he wore to arrive at the Brits) was a last-minute edition to my outfit. I plucked it from a chicken's arse on my way here." JUSTIN

"It's a case of greasing round the scrotum with Swarfega and shaving my buttocks so nothing catches on the fabric." JUSTIN

"Apparently we're the fastest-growing Brit band in the States since The Spice Girls. Maybe Geri's dress will prove an inspiration." JUSTIN

"Most of the comments I get aren't about my playing, it's all 'Oh I fucking love your guitar, mate'. If you disrespect it by smashing it, it's almost like slagging your wife off in a pub." JUSTIN

"Who wants to watch some bloke stand there in jeans and a T-shirt and just sing? Your image is your ambition." JUSTIN

"It's great that we can still divide people – we're obviously doing something right. I'm particularly pleased about being the worst-dressed star. Thanks to everyone who voted." JUSTIN

"I'm certain we would make it without the glam stuff but it wouldn't be as rewarding because the stuff I'm into is the high-impact stuff like Aerosmith with their big stadiums, pyrotechnics and flashy costumes. That's one of the reasons I'm doing this, I'm living the dream in a way." JUSTIN

"(Fashion) depends what sort of music you're playing. I mean Fred Durst in a catsuit wouldn't really work, as wouldn't Coldplay running around pulling guitar-hero poses! It's horses for courses really – I like my band to go for it on-stage or at least have the energy, to be excited by what we're doing. I think sometimes when bands plan things on-stage, that's when they fall on their arses – they either take themselves too seriously or it's actually some kind of joke! I think we get a good balance between the two." DAN

"I had a load of tattoos done before I was 18, which was a bit stupid. And I spent quite a lot of my early twenties not taking my clothes off. Then it got to the point where I thought 'fuck that' and I took my clothes off regardless." JUSTIN

"The thing that bothers me most about the rock scene is the baggy jeans because that's not *de rigueur* from when I was a kid listening to rock. But each to their own – it just means that they're up for conversion!" JUSTIN

CATSUITS & LIPSTICK

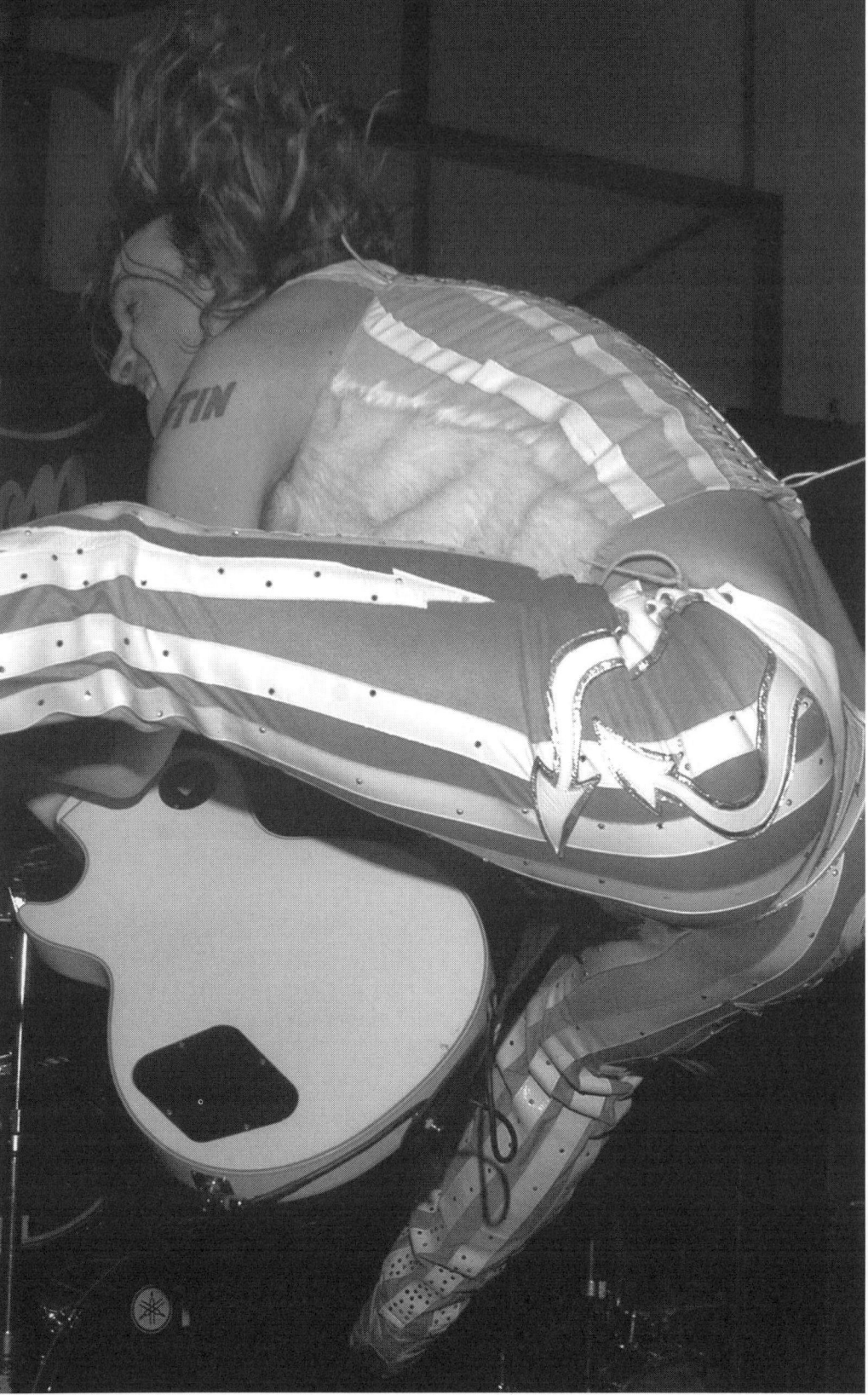

"I am constantly looking to improve the spectacle of our shows, and mostly my moves are the result of on-stage improvisation – I have a tailor, Christian Hutter, who creates my on-stage look(s) using his skill and imagination." JUSTIN

"Last week I bought a microphone costume. You wear it and sing through the mesh at the front. It's got a bow tie. That just speaks for itself, doesn't it? I had to have it 'cos I'm the singer, aren't I? Class!" JUSTIN

"Are we 'camp metal rockers'? I agree with the 'rockers' bit. People who say 'camp' are male. There is a correlation between how male you are and how jealous you are. (laughs) Men say 'you're camp', women say 'you're masculine'." JUSTIN

"I'm not wearing the white suit any more. I tried to do the splits in it but the arse split and one of my balls fell out on a TV show. It's irreparable now." JUSTIN

"During the gigs I keep a really close eye on what's going on. I also do Justin's costume change, which is a frenzied ripping-off his trousers to reveal the catsuit that lurks beneath. Sometimes it gets caught and there's a big tug-of-war going on backstage!"
TOM JENNINGS (JUSTIN'S TECH)

"You have to go commando in those things (catsuits). It's a question of how you avoid looking like you've just pulled your haemorrhoids forward, or when you get a stray testicle that wanders off to the right. They're a nuisance, those things." JUSTIN

"Because I wear silly clothes on stage, magazines always want to photograph me wearing them. The other day, we were taking some photos in a cafe and I was sitting at a table with my cup of tea wearing this pink and white catsuit. Everyone was staring!"
JUSTIN

CATSUITS & LIPSTICK

THE DARKNESS *Talking*

"Nowadays, rock means lots of things it never used to mean, like baggy trousers and skateboarding, whereas in the past it just meant having a good time in your tight jeans, with your long hair, not giving a fuck." **JUSTIN**

"My stage wardrobe is getting a big shake-up this year and there's a few things up my sleeve." **JUSTIN**

"It was always my ambition to be in a band that justified wearing costumes like I wear." **JUSTIN**

"This little zip-up number in orange leather and gold dots is worth around £3,000. I reckon we could auction it off for more than that because we could add a stupidity tax on top." **JUSTIN**

"When it comes to style and image and everything, it's only recently that we've had proper pictures taken. It's not something we're obsessed about, style and image. We approach it with a sense of enjoyment and fun, it's not something we sit down and seriously plan out." FRANKIE

"When we started the band we were like Meatloaf 'cos I was a big boy, a fat boy, y'know. With a combination of regular exercise and bulimia I managed to fight that. We all believe that we were born to do this and the people that liked us also thought that, so it's very clear that more people think that when you look like you were born to do it. We tried for ages to get Frankie to shave his moustache off – he's been cultivating that thing since middle school." JUSTIN

"We were like 'Come on Frankie, grow your hair, shave your moustache off', but he just wouldn't listen to us, and he was right. But I suppose the answer to the question of 'Is image important?' would be: 'Just look at me in these shorts with curry stains, cum stains, beer stains...'" JUSTIN

"At the end of the day we are not crude. People have this image of us. They think we're cock rock. It's time to rein it in a bit. We're not going, Wahey! and pouring champagne on girls' tits. That's embarrassing."
FRANKIE

CATSUITS & LIPSTICK

THE DARKNESS *Talking*

Just Justin

"My father worked his fingers to the bone as a builder, which is something he hated doing. He instilled in me that if you don't enjoy what you're doing, you'll end up miserable. If I wasn't enjoying something and doing something that was naturally fun, then that would be it. My happiness is the most important thing to me. Mine. Not anyone else's." **JUSTIN.**

"What's your favourite drink? That would be a Samoan Fog Cutter. It's a rum-related cocktail."
JUSTIN

"I can confirm that there is nothing freakish about my genitalia."
JUSTIN

"Am I tired with being called flamboyant? What other words are there? Whenever I see it, I don't feel disappointed." JUSTIN

❝I'd like to have been better at football. I never really played with all the other kids because I didn't like them. I regret that, really because I like to play in these celebrity five-a-side tournaments and it now transpires that I'm a bit shit.❞ JUSTIN

❝We wondered if people would approve of us going out, because she'd been managing me and Dan for seven years so we just kept it a secret. It was like we were having an illicit affair but it was just two people getting together. We fell in love... (then) the shit really hit the fan.

❝She's the best manager in the business (but) they wanted to sack her because we got together. And I said if you sack her you sack me, so none of us got sacked.❞

JUSTIN ON HIS RELATIONSHIP WITH SUE WHITEHOUSE

❝Me, Dan and Ed are depressive, and Justin's a manic depressive.❞

FRANKIE

❝Who would I prefer to be stranded on a desert island with – Kelly Osbourne or Avril Lavigne? If we were stranded for good, then there would be no point in going with Kelly (Osbourne), because I'm never going to meet her father. So I'll go with Avril.
It depends how big the island is, because I'd like my own section. And, obviously, if it came to having to forge a new race, then I would encroach on her half.❞ JUSTIN

❝When someone looks at that guitar (Les Paul) they should think of me.❞ JUSTIN

❝Justin generally has the one guitar change. He usually uses the 'Nugget' his Les Paul Gold Top reissue, for the first half of the gig, and then when he does his costume change he comes back on with the 'White Lady' as I call her – or the 'Alpine Slut', as he calls her!❞ TOM JENNINGS (JUSTIN'S TECH)

❝I'm an outstanding drummer, but mainly my resources go towards guitar.❞ JUSTIN

JUST JUSTIN

THE DARKNESS *Talking*

"Whatever you listen to, you sort of pick things up from it. You listen to stuff, it filters into techniques that you adopt, and what have you, and you drop things. I think when I started off I was probably a lot faster but not too melodic. I think I've become more melodic in my soloing with time." JUSTIN

"He dressed a bit like Austin Powers, or Mike Flowers, the spoof Sixties singer. He'd wear brown jackets with big lapels and he had a Jarvis Cocker hairdo. It wasn't until he took part in an end-of-year concert that his metal leanings came to the fore. Justin donned a long black wig to sing in his now-trademark falsetto for the fun gig. He was just like Ian Gillan from Deep Purple! It was outrageous!"
JUSTIN'S COLLEGE MUSIC TECHNOLOGY LECTURER CHARLIE GRIFFITHS

"In his head I think he sounds like Bon Scott and Steve Tyler, but where he sings most comfortably is really high – so what it's about is to do with not denying what you're good at rather than copying other people. If you were actually in the same room as Justin and heard his voice going up there, it's the loudest fucking thing you've ever heard!" DAN

"My folks are always on the phone wherever I am in the world, which is really nice." JUSTIN

"I've been in solitary confinement myself, when I went to Alkatraz (and) closed the door to give us a feel of what it was really like. I was in there with a few other people. So it wasn't really solitary. It was supposed to be this terrible dark experience but then this Japanese guy had his camera out and there were all these flashes going off!" JUSTIN

"When you hang out with Justin, that's what he's like – he's an attention-seeker, in the nicest possible way." ED

"At my funeral I'll have to be craned into the church, frozen in formaldehyde and riding a horse. Obviously the roof will have to be modified. Then there'll be a choir singing 'He rode a blazing saddle' with me on the horse, regardless of how fucked-up the injuries that resulted in my death were. I want people to be able to say 'What a wanker.'" JUSTIN

"Justin and I always do a vocal warm-up which is quite amusing if you're around, depending on the state of his voice on the day and what's he's been up to the previous night. We run scales, do all the breathing and give him little tips when his voice isn't working properly." TOM JENNINGS (JUSTIN'S TECH)

"I had a ghostly experience in the studio (Chapel). I was just having a little siesta and suddenly I was pinned to the bed and couldn't get up and there was this really loud noise in my ear, like a spaceship taking off or something. I ran downstairs, all hysterical, and went to phone my girlfriend. And then I woke up, and I wasn't near the phone, I wasn't hysterical and I could move. It's the weirdest thing I've experienced in my whole life. I think someone else said they'd had a funny experience there and it turns out they'd stayed in the same room as me. It is a chapel so there must be some kind of history to the place. It really shit me up, man!" JUSTIN

"Everything has it's price. Immortality in return for what? If they can package it with 'bigger cock' or something then maybe. And death is not the end, it's the beginning of a long and very peaceful sleep with no dreams." JUSTIN

"Justin never breaks a string. Nothing *ever* goes wrong for Justin Hawkins!" TOM JENNINGS (JUSTIN'S TECH)

JUST JUSTIN

Brotherly Love

"Justin was a show off, a total pain in the arse." DAN

"It's the same now, but it's not a school, it's a workplace. And the workplace is the realm of music. And it's benefited me greatly. And him (Dan)! So everyone's happy." JUSTIN

"I don't know who gets the most attention really – a bit of both. Dan's out more than me; I like to keep a low profile. Well when I'm out, I don't like to make a splash. I go to the ballet, opera, and seafood restaurants whereas Dan's always in the pub so he gets all the plebs!" JUSTIN

"I was born in Chertsey (Surrey) and my first memories are of my brother and pissing around with him. It was a happy childhood I think; a stable, nomadic family that was always keen to move to any area that was least likely to get hit by a bomb or which required the least streetwise-ness." JUSTIN

"Dan has always been the serious, hard-working one, a perfectionist if you like. Justin has just floated around and couldn't care less about any thing much, including school." SANDY HAWKINS

"My brother is the most driven person in rock, I go with the flow." JUSTIN

THE DARKNESS Talking

"I think that we realised that Dan and I could be a winning combination. A driven, serious person and a total twat." JUSTIN

"If Dan particularly wants to take a solo, I'm happy to stand aside and pose." JUSTIN

"Dan will get really pissed off because in a rehearsal we'll be jamming something out and he goes up to take the solo and I'm standing back trying to play some rhythm and it stops working because my rhythm playing is really bad. So then everyone just stops and Dan's like 'I'm playing a fucking solo, will you please continue?' It's the only time you really see him get pissed off. You can hear him thinking, 'Oh come on guys, does it have to be me that holds it together all the time?'" JUSTIN

"Basically, Justin's the best lead guitarist in the country at the moment." DAN

"Dan is a big strong man with a solid heart full of gold. When the shit hits the fan, Dan does carry the whole band, he is the driving force behind us. And I'm like the peripheral show-off that make it all a bit more glamorous." JUSTIN

"I seem to be the one who tells people off. But I try and make Justin's life as easy as possible. What he's got to do is important. And at any point he could go, 'Fuck it, I've had enough of this. I'm off to do something else.' I can see him walking away and not giving it a second thought." DAN

Ambition

"2003 has been a truly amazing year for us but we think there is a lot better to come." JUSTIN

"A Number 1 single and Number 1 album in America. That would be ideal. It's actually my next ambition in a way. We've had a Number 1 album in the UK and that was a really big thing for me. So now all we've got to do is do it in America and that will have the domino effect of doing it across the rest of the world." DAN

"So much has happened in a year. Everything is taking off all over the place and we head to America this summer (2004) to make a serious mark." JUSTIN

"Our album is selling well in America on import but Wal-Mart won't stock it because of the woman's bum on the sleeve. We'll just re-shoot it and turn the naked woman round so we can see her from the front instead!" FRANKIE

"I admit I am driven by a need to prove something to him, but I'm also doing it for my mum, who brought me up on my own. I will talk to him only after the Darkness have sold a million records."
FRANKIE ON HIS ABSENTEE FATHER

"There are territories around the world that won't take to us immediately. But we have great belief that, eventually, everyone around the planet will love us." JUSTIN

"We're going to make a fucking great second album that's going to be 10 times bigger and better than the first one. We've got a long career ahead of us and it's going to be great. Everyone's going to have a fucking great time. Trust me." DAN

AMBITION

THE DARKNESS *Talking*

JUSTIN WITH TARA PALMER TOMKINSON

"Our biggest ambition is to be the first band to play the rebuilt Wembley Stadium. We could've played in bigger venues on this tour. Indeed, a couple of the gigs have been upgraded, but we're not going to run before we can walk. We are looking to headline some festivals next year, though. And that's where we'll be able to introduce more pyrotechnics and put on the kind of show we really want to do. The aim is to give the fans something really special." FRANKIE

"Our fans are the best in the world – they don't need to be told that we're cool to be able to have a great time. When we started this band we had nothing – the music industry just didn't want to know, and because of our fans, the industry now recognises that we have the potential to succeed. We are nothing without you, sweet people of rock. Let's take over the fucking world together!" JUSTIN

"Why are we doing Robbie Williams' gigs at Knebworth? The simple answer is we can't turn down playing in front of half a million people!" FRANKIE

"We wanted a system where we could reward the people who stuck with us. That's why it took so long to get the deal through. Press, booking agents, distribution – we've stuck with them with this album. Atlantic were very understanding about the situation. It's a cut-throat business so it's nice to have a bit of humanity." FRANKIE

"My hope for 2004? Touring with Charlotte Church! We can but dream." JUSTIN

Conquering America

❝For 'Black Shuck', where I sing, 'That dog don't give a fuck!', I've changed it to 'duck'! I've got away with it too! You can either take the nonsensical approach to it all, or you can try doing something that still makes some sense. I prefer the nonsensical approach.❞
JUSTIN ON RE-RECORDING 'PERMISSION TO LAND' TO ENSURE DISTRIBUTION IN MAINSTREAM AMERICAN STORES

❝It's great that at our first New York show a bra was thrown at us.❞ JUSTIN

❝Usually at least four are thrown (bras), but this was our first time here and definitely a triumph.❞ FRANKIE

❝The intention (with my lyrics) was to just be myself and to speak honestly about things I want to speak about. Some people dumb down – they try to go global and eliminate regional references because they think people in America won't know what they're talking about.
❝But who cares if people in America don't know what they're talking about? If they want to know what you're talking about, they'll find out. There's a thing called the Internet and there's a whole resource of information available to everybody in all sorts of different forms.
❝If you're being yourself you don't get caught out and if you try and be global then you might do. I could be talking about Sunset Strip, but I've only been there twice so what do I know about it?❞
JUSTIN

> "I find the way to combat Americans is to take one step forward when they approach you. Square up to them." **DAN**

> "The only British bands that have made an impact here are the ones that toured relentlessly. And we've already made an impact, having played about 10 shows." **JUSTIN**

> "There's a magazine called *Blender* in the USA, it's basically their equivalent of *Q*, and their whole thing about the South by Southwest Festival was... quote 'there was one band there that was brilliant and they was The Darkness and they were the best!'" **JUSTIN**

> "They don't despise success over there (USA). All these indie no-marks go on about breaking America but they do one show in New York, don't like the drugs and want to come home. If you go out there and do the work, people will appreciate it and that's what The Darkness do. They work fucking hard." **IAN JOHNSEN, CO-FOUNDER OF MUST DESTROY MUSIC**

> "I might fly the flag for the country and get myself a Union Jack catsuit for our trip to America this year." **JUSTIN**

> "We've divided the public into people who either love us or hate us. And that percentage is about the same in the US as the UK: 90-10 against." **JUSTIN**

> "We're looking forward to hitting the Midwest, places like Pittsburgh that helped define rock music." **FRANKIE**

> "It's (America) very different to the UK, we didn't compromise at all in the UK, but over there you find that some people won't work with you unless you play things their way. It seems like you have to either kick people up the arse or kiss them on the arse to get them to respond to you." **JUSTIN**

CONQUERING AMERICA

THE DARKNESS *Talking*

> "I think rock is a nation in itself. It is one of the few genres that can transcend the cultural boundaries mankind puts in place. If you say certain parts of America are different animals to other ones, if you have a blunderbuss it's gonna hurt whether it's a weevil or an elephant. It's gonna hurt and it's gonna make some damage."
>
> **JUSTIN**

> "It's the biggest market around. It's happening – it'll happen. If it doesn't... People who say they haven't broken America, it's because they've stopped trying and we're going to keep trying."
>
> **JUSTIN**

> "America was the perfect market for The Darkness. In places like that they take the band at face value, think 'What amazing songs!' and then go and buy the album."
>
> **DARKNESS BOOKING AGENT RAD SAUNDERS**

> "At the time there was a lot of interest from the record companies, even though no-one knew what to do with the band. In the end, the gig (at Maggie Mae's in Austin, Texas) was packed out. I did the walkabout with Justin on my shoulders and the crowd wouldn't let me through. They just loved it."
>
> **PRODUCER PEDRO FERREIRA**

> "We're going over there (America) on a mission. We're proud to be British, we're proud of our roots. Music is apparently Britain's second biggest export after steel and it is important for us to fly the flag." **JUSTIN**

> "This is a band that has to be seen live and once they're out on the road, their fan base will increase hugely. We will be concentrating our efforts mainly in the US, but a lot of other territories will be covered, too." **SUE WHITEHOUSE**

> "I suppose you could say we are like athletes competing for Britain in America." **JUSTIN**

"It's all worked out very well. We had to work really hard in the UK, but things have gone totally to plan so now we can go to America with a great platform to start from. We're not arrogant, we're just incredibly ambitious. As soon as you start thinking you're the best thing since sliced bread it's all going to go pear-shaped." DAN

"'Growing On Me' was planned to be the (American) singles choice, but because of popular demand 'I Believe In A Thing Called Love' is going to be the first single released over there. It's on KROQ (a popular American radio station) already, so we're very pleased about that.

"As for touring, we're going to go back in two weeks. In November (2003) we'll be hitting places like Kansas and Detroit, then next year we're gonna hit those places properly and spend around four or five months there." FRANKIE

"There is a possibility of a support slot with Aerosmith and it would be nice to support AC/DC, although it's a tough gig that one, you know? You don't get any more passionate and loyal than the DC fans..." ED

"If this album gets to Number 1 in the States then that will be a real accomplishment. But we are aware that there will be a lot of touring involved. Whether that's as a support act or doing our own shows. Appearing on chat shows, like Jay Leno or David Letterman's wouldn't do any harm, either." FRANKIE

CONQUERING AMERICA

THE DARKNESS *Talking*

"I had to go to New York for a photo shoot and then go back to the UK the same day. I ended up being late for the shoot because immigration held me for an hour, asking me questions like 'Where were you on July 4?' and 'Have you ever been to Atlanta?' Apparently there's another bloke named Justin Hawkins who is from Atlanta and who looks a little like me, and he has done some bad things in his life and is on the most-wanted list. We're probably going to Atlanta on the next tour, which could be interesting." JUSTIN

"It just wasn't worth coming before. Playing America was always a priority, but say we did a show in Pittsburgh and no radio station played us. We wouldn't sell any tickets and it would be absolutely pointless. Now lots of stations have added our songs, so it's worth saying hello to those people." JUSTIN

"It will be nice to show people what we really do, because I think a lot of people see the video or hear one song on the radio and don't get the whole picture. We're actually a hard-rock band and we, like, rock hard." DAN

"They have the right attitude to succeed, specifically in the US. The States didn't get that whole Madchester and dance thing and now is the right time for a band such as The Darkness to break through there." EAST-WEST'S MANAGING DIRECTOR KORDA MARSHALL

"We played it one time, people hated it, saying 'What is this hair-metal crap?'. We stuck with it for a month and people went from 'It's not that bad' to 'I've got to hear it.' The Darkness have zigged where the rest of the music world has zagged and I believe they are less than a month away from crossing to pop." KROQ OPERATIONS MANAGER ROB CROSS

THE DARKNESS *Talking*

Crowd Control

"Our audience is getting younger as we're eventually becoming older, so it's not so much a case of scrotum stretching… but granted, we *are* a band who like our scrotums stretched!" ED

"In the current climate, in a culture where almost every musician is using his middle finger as a gesture, it's more rebellious to be positive and do the thumbs-up. And be positive and try and unite people, and to that extent that's become a punk gesture on one level.

"Also, if you're trying to encourage people to clap at the end, they're often holding a glass of beer in their teeth and that's dangerous. I wouldn't want to put our kids through that – we've got a responsibility to them. So one thumb's fine. Hold the glass carefully, don't spill it, don't drop it, don't roll around in broken glass. Just give us the thumbs-up and we'll be on our way." JUSTIN

"You learn from your mistakes. If we hadn't made those mistakes – at some point we'll make them on a much bigger scale. It would be nice to think that we've never embarrassed ourselves or done a shitty gig, but the fact is we have and we've learnt from it." JUSTIN

"It's always been important to us to get into big venues and play to a lot of people. That's what we've always been about." DAN

" (Disturbed's audience) had plastic bottles, but we had big bits of wood. Our techs had to be physically restrained from getting out there and kicking arse. I just wobbled my arse in their faces. It just made us do it more. When you're in a band, it's your job to divide people." JUSTIN

"Can you imagine how that went (supporting Disturbed)? They're huge in America; their gigs are like a religious experience. The singer's like (Waco cult leader) David Koresh, but he's three foot high and looks like a wrestler. Half the audience liked us and the other half was throwing bottles. I had coin marks on my knees; one bloke even threw his wallet. It was a really horrendous barrage of abuse. The first song went down really well, but as soon as I started singing it started to go badly wrong. I was tempted to smack them over the head with my guitar." JUSTIN

"They (the audience) expect to be a part of something and we deliver. It's a communal vibe that goes on. People want to connect with you, but they're still surprised... surprised they're enjoying themselves so much. Some people have attacked us for pandering to the crowd too much, but that's what we do! Some people think that's a bad thing. That shows you how bad music's got, bands think you should confront the audience." FRANKIE

"We've always been about reactions from the crowd, getting the crowd turned on. If people have their hands crossed, we see that as down to us not having done enough, as our responsibility..." ED

CROWD CONTROL

"We do pander to the crowd. We feed off their energy because you're only as good as the audience there to see you. If you have a good time at the show, you'll want to go again." JUSTIN

"We've spent nearly four years playing clubs and sports halls trying to get where we are, so we understand that, even when a gig looks like it's going shit, you can be stood there with two people who are hating it, but the person behind might be really into it but feel intimidated about getting into the music because the others might turn around and start beating you up! So you play for the people you imagine are into it – you can't be selfish." DAN

"I used to hand-pick a different member from the audience. I'd choose them beforehand to the show, and say, 'You are the chosen one... for the walk-about.' It was like a knighthood. Only instead of a sword, I'd have my... *Erm*, you know. But most of the time now, it's our sound-bloke (Pedro), who produced our album, that carries me, because he's got broad shoulders. He's not averse to having a sweaty old scrotum against his neck." JUSTIN

"We're the band the public want because they've created us, in a strange way. We feed off their energy, so we think about what will make them go crazy. That's why our live shows have become successful. There are loads of bands out there that are just happy to imitate or even stare at their feet the whole time. They think it's insulting or arrogant to put on a great show or keep people happy. And they think their lack of ambition is cool?" FRANKIE

"We've got a real cross-section: grannies in deckchairs, five-year-olds in pushchairs. People who haven't got chairs at all sometimes! We have a much wider appeal than we expected." JUSTIN

CROWD CONTROL

THE DARKNESS *Talking*

A Thing Called Fame

"Fame comes at a price, but it pays dividends in other areas. You have to take the rough with the smooth." **JUSTIN**

"It was a hand-written letter, it's very weird. It's quite flattering that somebody wants to kill me, but at the same time it's very scary. I'm more concerned about my own safety really. You can't go on being nice to everybody because sometimes people take the piss and they start to take liberties."
JUSTIN, ON RECEIVING A DEATH THREAT

"Last year I had to borrow 30 quid off a mate for Christmas because I'd been starving and I thought it was time to go home and get fed. This year I'm employing 45 people. It's mental." **DAN**

"There's never any time to sit around sucking each others' cocks." FRANKIE

"It's responsibility that you have to keep your eye out for. There are people that come up and ask for us to sign things, or who have a tattoo of our logo on their arm, which demonstrates the fact we have people whose lives we have changed. To that extent, that's quite a head-spinning thing to fathom. But once you realise you owe these people something, you can't fuck it up. The fans are like our kids in that sense, and we can't let them down. Because otherwise they've got the logo of a shit band on their arm. It would also be wrong for us to change our logo now, as well..."
JUSTIN

"I'm a bit of a softy but I guess you have to draw the line eventually. You just humour people to a degree. Dan would probably be quite firm about (weeding out hangers-on), while Ed is very accommodating. Only last night he brought a big group of people from the pub back to his house – he's like a John Bonham/Keith Moon type." FRANKIE

"I had a really great time (at the launch party for *Permission To Land*). The only thing that got me was the fact that the air hostess bar staff didn't recognise me when I went to the bar and the guests in the VIP area were more famous than me!" JUSTIN

"I'm looking into getting my own helicopter and train myself up as a pilot. It costs about £50,000 a year to hire a pilot on retainer so you may as well buy (a 'copter) and fly it yourself. Cool for arriving at festivals."
DAN

A THING CALLED FAME

THE DARKNESS *Talking*

"The money is coming in a bit now but it's been hard. My mum and dad had to remortgage their house to keep us going. Their only condition was we buy them a swimming pool if we make it." DAN

"I like to sit in a pub and just talk to someone and I've got a few mates I can still do that with. But often it's just 'You're Number 1' or 'Your music…' After a while you don't really want to talk about it. If you're a plumber you don't want to sit and talk about copper fucking piping. So I tend to go to the ballet or the opera or the fifth floor at Harvey Nic's or a cocktail bar and just sit there and drink, on my own, staring sorrowfully into the bottom of my margarita glass." JUSTIN

"What does scare me is, when I'm super-famous, people outside my house in their pants, polishing their shotguns." JUSTIN

"**The unveiling of the Darkness ASCAR (drag racer) was an emotional moment – four wheels of fury, primed to race that baby in a one-way journey to hell and back.**" JUSTIN

"We're just not coping with all this attention. I thought we were coping, but I'm not. We are rotating at a rapid rate, we haven't really got a chance to sit down and appreciate it. When the ride stops we'll all be giddy." JUSTIN

"**It's daunting when you look at your diary and you realise you've nothing in the way of a day off. Then again there are plumbers who are fully booked, and then you get emergency call-outs on top of that. It's impossible to fathom until the shit really hits the fan… and that we will be when I fake my death.**" JUSTIN

"What have I blown my advance on? I'm having a white patent-leather suit made… mostly see-through! Hee hee hee! But I haven't made any stupid, large purchases (with my advance). I got myself a new gold guitar, but that's it." JUSTIN

"**You spend years on the dole, watching daytime TV, dreaming of this moment. So we're getting really stuck into it and working our arses off. Maybe on the schedule there's like two weeks off for Christmas and that's it for the next two years – but that suits me."** DAN

"**I've never had enough respect for the industry to let it change me in any way. At the moment it seems like everything we touch turns to gold, but there'll come a time when that changes... but we won't change with it, we'll keep doing what we're doing."** JUSTIN

"**Basically, we signed a record deal and we all got given a certain amount of money to get ourselves out of debt. I'm still skint, whereas these guys only had a couple of hundred pounds' debt and have got loads of money. So to console myself I decide – right – I'm going to go on the Internet and find the coolest-looking guitar. I'm going to order it and buy it and no-one is going to argue with me. So I went onto the Gretsch website 'cos I've always liked Gretsches even though I always thought they looked a bit old-school and sound a bit honking sometimes. But I found the fucking coolest guitar I'd ever seen and it was that Elliot Easton thing. It's like a Les Paul, but the Pat Butcher of fucking Les Pauls; it's dripping with gold, yeah?"** DAN

"**Blow me away and make me a three-and-a-half-grand guitar. And make it look as much like a Les Paul as you can. With Washburn written on it. It will have pink and black stripes like a tiger and thunderbolts like my tattoo as fret markings, and it will have a synthesiser attached to it as well."** JUSTIN

A THING CALLED FAME

THE DARKNESS *Talking*

> "You know when you're so busy you don't watch TV or read the papers... it's a saving grace in a way. Because, if you were just reading about yourself, you'd probably get over-inflated." FRANKIE

> "This time last year I was a music nobody. Today I sit at the top of the music tree, feeling pretty good. A major highlight of 2003 was when we headlined Knebworth with Mr Robbie Williams as our warm-down act. Despite the fact that we upstaged him in a pretty dramatic way, Robbie was extremely gracious in accepting a lesson in rock, administered by The Darkness – until the point that his cool friends turned up, that is, and he dropped us like a hot potato." JUSTIN

> "It doesn't feel real because we haven't had any time to sit down and think, 'Fuckin' hell, we're famous!' It's only when we're travelling to new places, and we see the response when we go onstage that we really realise we're part of a phenomenon. No-one saw this one coming, did they?" JUSTIN

> "I think I'll spend some of the money on patenting a Darkness whelk-clam trident. I want to rush that idea through and get them on the merchandise stall as soon as possible. I want to get a little workshop somewhere and start churning them out. I'm going to buy a shark too. I'll get an enormous tank built for it and just sit there watching it, smoking." JUSTIN

> "Success has brought a certain amount of responsibility. I've met the fans of the band who tell us we've changed their lives... The responsibility can be overwhelming, and that's why it's important to still do normal things from time to time. Like go swimming." JUSTIN

THE DARKNESS *Talking*

Famous Followers...

> "Many people are calling them a throwback...to the Led Zeppelin era. But for today, they are wildly unique. Part of the fun with The Darkness is the debate: can it be fun and funny and be legitimate and serious? The Darkness is the answer to that."
>
> RON SHAPIRO, ATLANTIC RECORDS CO-PRESIDENT

> "At first there was a bit of weirdness between us and them in London. Our songs were on the radio at the same time and we kept them out of the Number 1 spot for about seven weeks. They are from the UK. It felt kind of weird. We didn't gel at first. The more we saw them at awards ceremonies and big awards we kind of joked around with them and became acquaintants. So on this tour its like 'Hey, what's up Justin?' and he said we should do a song together. I thought 'A song with The Darkness? That would be pretty cool.' He comes up to me and said he wanted to jump on stage with us, so I told him to come on during 'Retarded' because that is the perfect song." WILL I AM, BLACK EYED PEAS

> "I first saw them play at the Monarch in Camden. I loved the band straight away. Every time I had some spare time I hung out with them and it progressed from there. They're great to work with. I have such a great time being around them."
>
> PRODUCER PEDRO FERREIRA

> "They came on and me and my girlfriend stood there with our jaws on the floor. We couldn't stop talking about them afterwards."
>
> IAN JOHNSEN, CO-FOUNDER OF MUST DESTROY MUSIC

"They know what they're doing isn't Shakespeare, but it is different to anything else around, and that is its true value. It is the start of a new generation of fun music... like watching AC/DC meets Queen fronted by the singer from Sparks."

DEF LEPPARD'S JOE ELLIOTT

DEF LEPPARD'S JOE ELLIOTT

"Those gigs at the Monarch (pub in Camden, London) were amazing. To start with it was just friends who came, but as time went on we started getting other people in. At one show it was so full you could feel the floor shaking." PEDRO FERREIRA

"I'm a massive Darkness fan. I saw them play one song at Reading this year and I was totally won over, really impressed. I don't have the album yet but I've seen the videos and I'm definitely a fan. It's like a time warp that's going on. You really do feel like you've just stepped out of a time machine with them. And I can't help but be impressed by the high notes that he hits, it's like Freddie Mercury. The lead singer draws you in. You have to appreciate what they're doing. I don't know if they'll make it in America, but why not? They're charismatic enough, so I think they've got a good shot."

YEAH YEAH YEAHS SINGERS KAREN O

"Me and my business partner used to do a club night in Notting Hill, so we put The Darkness on. That was our only real business with the band until Sue Whitehouse (the band's manager) called us and asked if we wanted to put a single out on the label we'd just got together. That was an easy decision. We didn't think about success, we just wanted to put this fucking great record out." IAN JOHNSEN, CO-FOUNDER OF MUST DESTROY MUSIC

FAMOUS FOLLOWERS...

THE DARKNESS Talking

> I started working with them straight after I saw them for the first time at the Notting Hill Arts Club. It was obvious that they were special. I had a meeting with them two days later and said 'I have to be your agent' over and over again. I wouldn't let them leave until they agreed. **BOOKING AGENT RAD SAUNDERS**

> I saw the Darkness playing at a *Jackass* party in London and thought they were just the wildest thing. There's no-one else out there with the balls and fearlessness to do what they do. I think they will blow America apart.
> BAM MARGERA, SKATEBOARDER & MTV PRESENTER

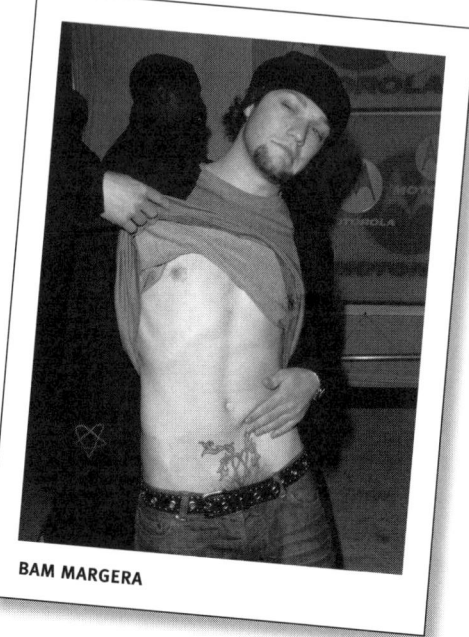

BAM MARGERA

> When 'I Believe In A Thing Called Love' first came out I was really curious because it was so different to everything else. Then I saw them play at an XFM gig and they blew me away. I came in the next day and put them on the playlist. Then we started talking with the band about how we could support them more and break them onto Radio 1.
> XFM RADIO HEAD OF MUSIC ANDY ASHTON

> I came into work and one of our music guys played the single to me, saying that I'd either love it or hate it. My first reaction was 'What the fuck?' I went down to the studio and played it again really fucking loud, and absolutely loved it. I played it on the show the same day. Some people thought they were a joke band, but I felt it was really important to make the point

"that they were real and all about making great music. **We made it our record of the week and hammered it, with loads of air guitar going on in the studio.**" RADIO 1 DJ JO WHILEY

"Before the album ('Permission To Land') came out they'd done dates with Whitesnake, Deep Purple, Def Leppard and Alice Cooper. It worked really well for us because, to be honest, there wasn't much competition for those support slots. The Darkness can play with anybody. I don't think there's another act in the country that could play with both Metallica and Robbie Williams." BOOKING AGENT RAD SAUNDERS

"**Justin phoned me in the autumn and joked about funding a new recording studio for us. But he did say he'd love to come back and talk to the students sometime. We're thrilled to bits that the Darkness have done so well and Justin's welcome to drop in and see us whenever he wants!**" JUSTIN'S TUTOR RICK COCKE

"They deserve everything they get because they work their bollocks off. They're like four real-life David Lee Roths. They're fucking armour-plated. There's not an ego between them and they work like cunts. All these people who've got a problem with them are just lazy fuckers. And The Darkness have got hair! All those nu-metal cunts were fucking bald!" WILDHEARTS FRONTMAN GINGER

"**Just like after Oasis played in the King Tut's Tent in 1994, this year over 50,000 people have been claiming that they watched The Darkness open T in the Park in 2003 before they were famous!**" T IN THE PARK'S GEOFF ELLIS

"It's not a record you can play as background music. I couldn't believe Justin Hawkins was singing the way he was until I sat down and listened to it again! It's like Queen meets Aerosmith meets Thin Lizzy. My bandmate the Fox (Dan Edwards) lost his mind over it! America will *love* this band!" JOHNNY MILLION OF CHICAGO ROCKERS THE MILLIONS

FAMOUS FOLLOWERS...

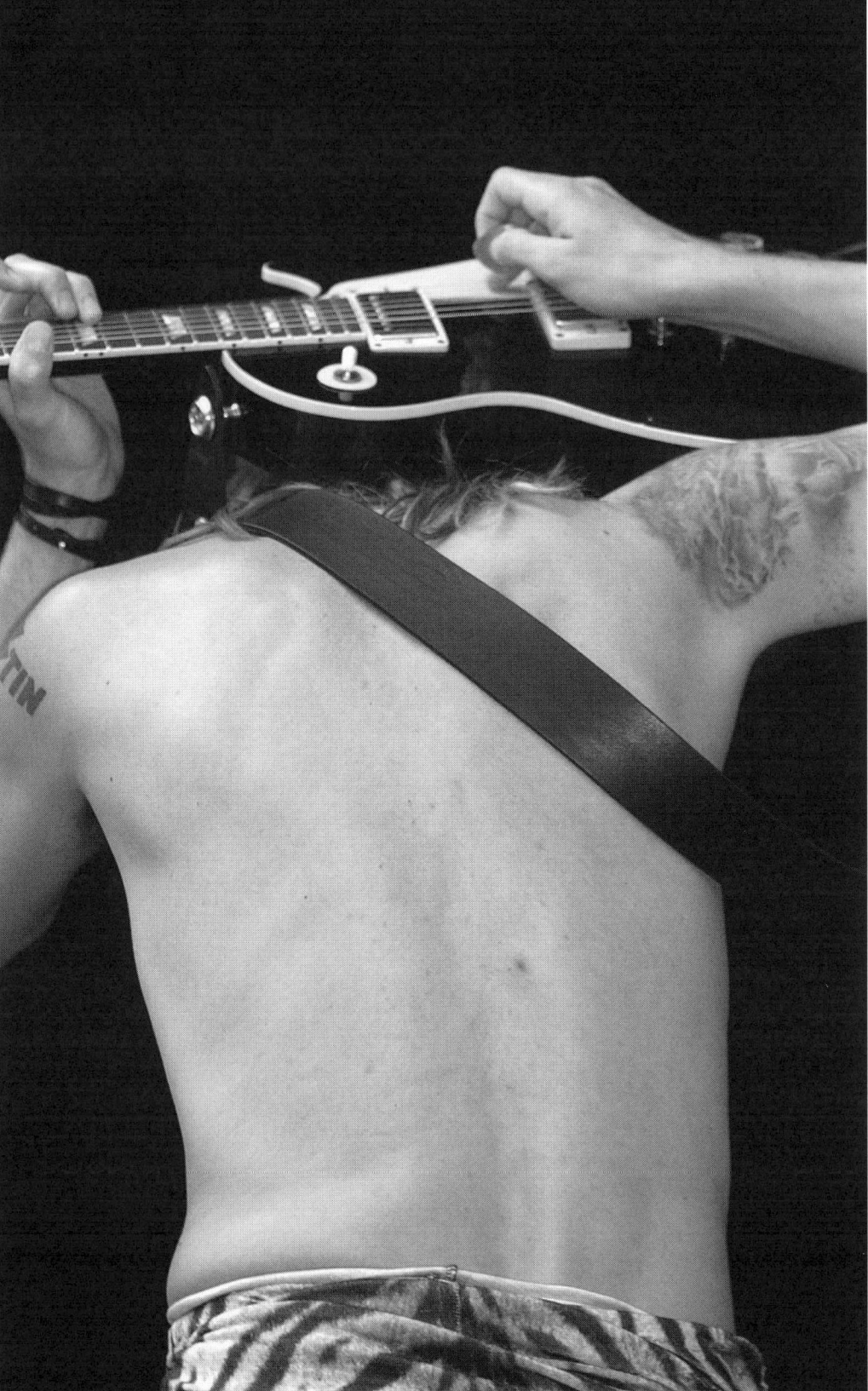

Future

"We're going to rock the whole world to its foundations... actually, that's not a secret. That's fact." **FRANKIE**

"It's nice to be where we are, but we're nowhere near happy yet. Once we're an internationally huge rock band and generally playing stadiums, then I think we'll be getting there, you know?" **JUSTIN**

"A lot of people say 'how does it feel to have come so far?', but it's hard to say how we feel. If it was a musical feeling, you know, we'd probably feel like 'Nothing's Gonna Stop Us Now', like Jefferson Starship. Not that I'm the expert on Jefferson Starship, I've not studied their back catalogue or anything." **FRANKIE**

"We've done all our modesty now; it's time for us to crack on. The truth is, we are as good, if not better, than many of today's top acts. Crisp and true, the sound of champions running through." **JUSTIN**

"People say we'll be gone in six months, but we'll be conquering Andorra by then." **DAN**

"We are the revolution and have been sent to pull rock from its own arsehole." **FRANKIE**

"We don't want to become a coffee-table band like the Lighthouse Family, where you go, 'Oh, I like that new album. I don't love it. But I'll bloody well buy it anyway.'" **JUSTIN**

THE DARKNESS *Talking*

"We've got another side project to be working on too. It's songs for people in prison, like 'You Look Like A Girl From Behind And That's Enough' and 'Coffin Bomber', which is the tale of a man who went to prison, came out and killed the jury, went back inside for 10 years and then came out and decided that the jury wasn't dead enough and bombed all their coffins. It's loosely based on a true story. It's actually about the sinking of the *Titanic*. We've got another prison song, too, about being in solitary. It's called 'You Should Get Out More'. I don't suppose they'll get to hear it. You don't get stereos in solitary, do you? They might pipe it through the tannoy system, though..." JUSTIN

"We've got a busy year. There are a lot of people who go, 'Oh you know, we can see it works for one record, where's it going to go for the next?'" DAN

"We'll be doing British festivals too. Watch this space. There's more to come." JUSTIN

"We'd like to do an album every year. I don't want to be a one-album band. I don't want to tour relentlessly with an album that doesn't represent where we are now." JUSTIN

"I think we're going to give the big boys a run for their money."
JUSTIN

"Next year (2004) we're going to be doing one of the biggest arena tours of the last 15 or 20 years, the next album is going to be released and we'll enter the classic albums territory rather than being this phenomena. And one of the ways you go about that is by becoming internationally massive." DAN

"When the backlash comes it's going to be intense, because people really got behind us this year (2003). The only way to make next year better is to get another album out. Or we could just keep gigging this album forever and disappear into obscurity. I don't like that choice much, though." JUSTIN

"Once they've rebuilt Wembley and renamed it the Darkness Stadium, we'll play there and I'll be fired onstage as a human cannonball. I'll hit the wall, slide down and start the first track." JUSTIN

"There was no masterplan there really... it kind of works on a subliminal level, as it's something we all talk about and agree on, like a light bulb goes off in one of our heads and we all latch onto it. If we don't latch onto it, we don't do it. It's just one of these streams of consciousness elements that runs through our career. Hopefully it's gonna carry on – and hopefully we're here to stay for a while." ED

"This is just the start of the journey. There's a long way to go. We haven't really explored other countries enough yet." FRANKIE

"You haven't even seen the tip of the iceberg. It's the tip of the tip. It's like a snowflake atop the iceberg... The question is how many snowflakes does it take to build an iceberg? And only the Lord above can answer that because he's the one who makes them." JUSTIN

FUTURE